The Gospel According to Mark
Part Two

The Gospel According to Mark
Part Two

Mark 9:33–16:20

Marie Noonan Sabin
with Little Rock Scripture Study staff

LITURGICAL PRESS
Collegeville, Minnesota

www.littlerockscripture.org

Nihil obstat for the commentary text by Marie Noonan Sabin: Robert C. Harren, *Censor deputatus.*
Imprimatur for the commentary text by Marie Noonan Sabin: ✠ John F. Kinney, Bishop of St. Cloud, Minnesota, December 2, 2005.

Cover design by John Vineyard. Interior art by Ned Bustard. Map on page 10 created by Ann Blattner. Map on page 59 created by Clifford M. Yeary with Ann Blattner. Illustration on page 80 courtesy of Getty Images.

Scripture texts in this work are taken from the *New American Bible, revised edition* © 2010, 1991, 1986, 1970; *New American Bible with Revised New Testament and Revised Psalms* © 1991, 1986, 1970 (where noted) Confraternity of Christian Doctrine, Washington, D.C. and are used by permission of the copyright owner. All Rights Reserved. No part of the New American Bible may be reproduced in any form without permission in writing from the copyright owner.

 This symbol indicates material that was created by Little Rock Scripture Study to supplement the biblical text and commentary. Some of these inserts first appeared in the *Little Rock Catholic Study Bible*; others were created specifically for this book by Catherine Upchurch and Michael DiMassa.

Commentary by Marie Noonan Sabin © 2006, 2020 by Order of Saint Benedict, Collegeville, Minnesota. Inserts adapted from *Little Rock Catholic Study Bible*, © 2011 by Little Rock Scripture Study, Little Rock, Arkansas; additional inserts, prayers, and study questions by Little Rock Scripture Study staff, © 2020 by Order of Saint Benedict, Collegeville, Minnesota. All rights reserved. No part of this book may be used or reproduced in any manner whatsoever, except brief quotations in reviews, without written permission of Liturgical Press, Saint John's Abbey, PO Box 7500, Collegeville, MN 56321-7500. Printed in the United States of America.

1   2   3   4   5   6   7   8   9

Library of Congress Cataloging-in-Publication Data

Names: Sabin, Marie Noonan, author. | Little Rock Scripture Study Staff, author.
Title: The gospel according to Mark / Marie Noonan Sabin with Little Rock Scripture Study staff.
Description: Collegeville : Liturgical Press, 2020. | Includes commentary from author's previously published work and excerpts adapted from Little Rock Catholic Study Bible. | Contents: Part one: Mark 1-9:32 — Part two: Mark 9:33-16. | Summary: "A Bible study of the Gospel According to Mark. Part One covers Mark 1:1-9:32, providing an in-depth study of Jesus' ministry of healing and preaching. Part Two explores Mark 9:33-16:20, including Jesus' entry into Jerusalem and the events of his passion, death, and resurrection. Commentary, study and reflection questions, prayers, and access to online lectures are included for each volume"— Provided by publisher.
Identifiers: LCCN 2020000472 (print) | LCCN 2020000473 (ebook) | ISBN 9780814665190 (paperback) | ISBN 9780814665442 (paperback) | ISBN 9780814665206 (v. 1 ; epub) | ISBN 9780814665206 (v. 1 ; mobi) | ISBN 9780814665206 (v. 1 ; pdf) | ISBN 9780814665459 (v. 2 ; epub) | ISBN 9780814665459 (v. 2 ; mobi) | ISBN 9780814665459 (v. 2 ; pdf)
Subjects: LCSH: Bible. Mark—Textbooks.
Classification: LCC BS2586 .S23 2020 (print) | LCC BS2586 (ebook) | DDC 226.3/077—dc22
LC record available at https://lccn.loc.gov/2020000472
LC ebook record available at https://lccn.loc.gov/2020000473

TABLE OF CONTENTS

Welcome	7
What materials will you use?	8
How will you use these materials?	8
Map of Palestine	10
Lesson One (Introduction and Mark 9:33–10:52)	11
Lesson Two (Mark 11–12)	29
Lesson Three (Mark 13–14)	45
Lesson Four (Mark 15–16)	67
Praying with Your Group	90
Reflecting on Scripture	92

 Wrap-Up Lectures and Discussion Tips for Facilitators are available for each lesson at no charge. Find them online at LittleRockScripture.org/Lectures/MarkPartTwo.

Welcome

The Bible is at the heart of what it means to be a Christian. It is the Spirit-inspired word of God for us. It reveals to us the God who created, redeemed, and guides us still. It speaks to us personally and as a church. It forms the basis of our public liturgical life and our private prayer lives. It urges us to live worthily and justly, to love tenderly and wholeheartedly, and to be a part of building God's kingdom here on earth.

Though it was written a long time ago, in the context of a very different culture, the Bible is no relic of the past. Catholic biblical scholarship is among the best in the world, and in our time and place, we have unprecedented access to it. By making use of solid scholarship, we can discover much about the ancient culture and religious practices that shaped those who wrote the various books of the Bible. With these insights, and by praying with the words of Scripture, we allow the words and images to shape us as disciples. By sharing our journey of faithful listening to God's word with others, we have the opportunity to be stretched in our understanding and to form communities of love and learning. Ultimately, studying and praying with God's word deepens our relationship with Christ.

The Gospel According to Mark, Part Two
Mark 9:33–16:20

The resource you hold in your hands is divided into four lessons. Each lesson involves personal prayer and study using this book *and* the experience of group prayer, discussion, and wrap-up lecture.

If you are using this resource in the context of a small group, we suggest that you meet four times, discussing one lesson per meeting. Allow about 90 minutes for the small group gathering. Small groups function best with eight to twelve people to ensure good group dynamics and to allow all to participate as they wish.

Some groups choose to have an initial gathering before their regular sessions begin. This allows an opportunity to meet one another, pass out books, and, if desired, view the optional intro lecture for this study available on the "Resources" page of the Little Rock Scripture Study website (www.littlerockscripture.org). Please note that there is only one intro lecture for two-part studies.

Every Bible study group is a little bit different. Some of our groups like to break each lesson up into two weeks of study so they are reading less each week and have more time to discuss the questions together at their weekly gatherings. If your group wishes to do this, simply agree how much of each lesson will be read each week, and only answer the questions that correspond to the material you read. Wrap-up lectures can then be viewed at the end of every other meeting rather than at the end of every meeting. Of course, this will mean that your study will last longer, and your group will meet more times.

WHAT MATERIALS WILL YOU USE?

The materials in this book include:

- The text of the Gospel of Mark, chapters 9:33–16:20, using the New American Bible, Revised Edition as the translation.
- Commentary by Marie Noonan Sabin (which has also been published separately as part of the New Collegeville Bible Commentary series).
- Occasional inserts 🔥 highlighting elements of the chapters of Mark being studied. Some of these appear also in the *Little Rock Catholic Study Bible* while others are supplied by staff writers.
- Questions for study, reflection, and discussion at the end of each lesson.
- Opening and closing prayers for each lesson, as well as other prayer forms available in the closing pages of the book.

In addition, there are wrap-up lectures available for each lesson. Your group may choose to purchase a DVD containing these lectures or make use of the audio or video lectures online at no charge. The link to these free lectures is: LittleRockScripture.org/Lectures/MarkPartTwo. Of course, if your group has access to qualified speakers, you may choose to have live presentations.

Each person will need a current translation of the Bible. We recommend the *Little Rock Catholic Study Bible*, which makes use of the New American Bible, Revised Edition. Other translations, such as the New Jerusalem Bible or the New Revised Standard Version: Catholic Edition, would also work well.

HOW WILL YOU USE THESE MATERIALS?

Prepare in advance

Using Lesson One as an example:

- Begin with a simple prayer like the one found on page 11.

- Read the assigned material in the printed book for Lesson One (pages 12–24) so that you are prepared for the weekly small group session. You may do this assignment by reading a portion over a period of several days (effective and manageable) or by preparing all at once (more challenging).
- Answer the questions, Exploring Lesson One, found at the end of the assigned reading, pages 25–26.
- Use the Closing Prayer on page 27 when you complete your study. This prayer may be used again when you meet with the group.

Meet with your small group
- After introductions and greetings, allow time for prayer (about 5 minutes) as you begin the group session. You may use the prayer found on page 11 (also used by individuals in their preparation) or use a prayer of your choosing.
- Spend about 45–50 minutes discussing the responses to the questions that were prepared in advance. You may also develop your discussion further by responding to questions and interests that arise during the discussion and faith-sharing itself.
- Close the discussion and faith-sharing with prayer, about 5–10 minutes. You may use the Closing Prayer at the end of each lesson or one of your choosing at the end of the book. It is important to allow people to pray for personal and community needs and to give thanks for how God is moving in your lives.
- Listen to or view the wrap-up lecture associated with each lesson (15–20 minutes). You may watch the lecture online, use a DVD, or provide a live lecture by a qualified local speaker. This lecture provides a common focus for the group and reinforces insights from each lesson. You may view the lecture together at the end of the session or, if your group runs out of time, you may invite group members to watch the lecture on their own time after the discussion.

Above all, be aware that the Holy Spirit is moving within and among you.

Palestine in the Time of Jesus

The Gospel According to Mark

Part Two

LESSON ONE

Introduction and Mark 9:33–10:52

Begin your personal study and group discussion with a simple and sincere prayer such as:

Prayer

Lord Jesus, as we read this Gospel, may we hear your words and meditate on your life with open hearts and alert minds. May our time of study and sharing strengthen our faith in you, the source of all truth and wisdom.

Read the Introduction on pages 12–13 and the Bible text of Mark 9:33–10:52 found in the outside columns of pages 15–23, highlighting what stands out to you.

Read the accompanying commentary to add to your understanding.

Respond to the questions on pages 25–26, Exploring Lesson One.

The Closing Prayer on page 27 is for your personal use and may be used at the end of group discussion.

Lesson One

INTRODUCTION

Welcome to Part Two of Little Rock Scripture Study's *The Gospel According to Mark*. Before we begin our in-depth study of Mark 9:33–16:20, let's review some of the pertinent themes of Mark's Gospel that appeared in the first half of the study. These themes will continue to be of importance throughout the second half of Mark.

First, our commentator Marie Noonan Sabin encourages us to encounter Jesus in Mark's Gospel as a wisdom teacher rooted in the Hebrew wisdom tradition. This is a core tradition that Jesus both enriches and enhances. In the first half of Mark, Jesus' wisdom is most clearly seen in his parables, which begin with three parables concerning seeds (4:1-34). While Jesus teaches the crowds that gather around him, he also calls specific people like Peter, James, and John to follow him throughout his ministry. Throughout the Gospel, these disciples show real difficulty in understanding Jesus' true identity. In Mark 8:29 Jesus asks his disciples the all-important question of the Gospel: "But who do you say that I am?" This is a question that all who study the Gospel of Mark should ask themselves.

As we move into the second half of Mark, it is also important to bear in mind how Peter responds to Jesus' question and how Jesus, in turn, responds to Peter. Peter confidently tells Jesus: "You are the Messiah." But Jesus' response to this affirmation is to warn Peter not to tell anyone (8:30). Jesus knows that Peter does not yet fully understand his own declaration. In Mark, Jesus' disciples fail to grasp that the cross is at the heart of Jesus' identity, even though he explicitly warns them throughout the Gospel that his mission will lead to his crucifixion. The cross is not only at the heart of his own mission, but those who follow him must take up their own crosses and be willing to endure persecution (4:17; 10:30).

The failure of Jesus' disciples to understand the centrality of the cross is due in part to their expectation that Jesus, being the Messiah, will establish himself with power in Israel. Hoping for a share in that power, they compete with each other in establishing their own importance. Part One of our study ended with Mark 9:30-32, where Jesus warned the disciples once again of his impending passion. And of course, the disciples yet again failed to understand what that would mean. We now begin Part Two with Mark 9:33-37, where Jesus seeks to show the disciples that authentic humility and meekness are required in order to be considered "first" among his followers.

As you begin your study of Part Two of *The Gospel According to Mark*, it is our hope that you will enter this study as a seeker of divine wisdom, carrying with you a keen desire to see more clearly who Jesus is and who he calls his followers to be.

NOTES ON THE TRANSLATION

Literal or root meanings

The Church encourages translators to return to "the original texts of the sacred books" (*Dogmatic Constitution on Divine Revelation*, 22). That recommendation has been followed scrupulously in this commentary, to the point where the commentator often renders the meaning of the biblical words and phrases in a more literal way than the NABRE translation provided. This kind of conscious choice, while found throughout the commentary in the author's own translations, is particularly evident in four key words that will be explored in the commentary: "release," "rise up" or "raised up," "straightway," and "ecstasy" or "ecstatic." These and other words translated by the author will be clearly marked with asterisks throughout the commentary.

Capitalization

In some instances, the difference between the commentator's translation and that of the NABRE involves capitalization. The reader should know that we have no original manuscripts of the Gospels, and that of those we do possess, the best were written entirely in capital letters called "uncials." Thus all modern capitals are the choice of a later editor. Such editorial emendations are, like translations, forms of interpretation. This commentator has chosen not to capitalize certain words in order to highlight what she believes to be Mark's theological view.

For example, she does not capitalize "son of man" because she believes that it is not used by Mark as a special title, but rather in its usual Hebrew sense of *ben ʿadam,* which literally means "son of Adam" or "human being." (She also sees it as sometimes following the Aramaic custom of using it as an alternative to "I.") She believes that Mark's habit of constantly associating the term with Jesus expresses his theological perception of Jesus as a second Adam. She does not capitalize "messiah" because she wants to emphasize that Mark redefined that term in the process of using it, and she would like to encourage the reader to reflect on that redefinition. She does not capitalize "holy spirit" because she wants to remind the reader of its use throughout the Hebrew Bible. While the modern Christian of course sees this phrase in relation to the Trinitarian understanding of the fourth-century creed, Mark's first-century audience would have heard it in terms of the biblical tradition they knew.

Lesson One

NEW PERCEPTIONS

Mark 9:33-50

9:33-37 "Who is the greatest?"

Mark underlines the disciples' lack of understanding in the next episode. We have seen how twice before, Mark has shown Jesus telling these disciples that he must be rejected, suffer, and die (8:31; 9:31). He has shown Jesus making an explicit connection between his cross and their discipleship (8:34-35). And yet here they are, "discussing among themselves . . . who was the greatest" (9:34).

Mark indicates that they had some sense of the inappropriateness of their discussion by noting that they did not answer Jesus' question but "remained silent" (9:34). Mark then uses their question to set up further teaching by Jesus: "If anyone wishes to be first, he shall be the last of all and the servant of all" (9:35).

It is worth noting that Jesus "called the Twelve" before giving this teaching. This is the third time that Jesus summons and instructs the Twelve; in effect, it is another Markan triad. The first time, Jesus sends them out as apostles "to preach and to have authority to drive out demons" (3:14-15); the second time, he instructs them "to take nothing for the journey but a walking stick" (6:8); here he instructs them to be servants. Mark shows Jesus pro-

> **IV: The Full Revelation of the Mystery**
>
> *The Greatest in the Kingdom*
>
> ³³They came to Capernaum and, once inside the house, he began to ask them, "What were you arguing about on the way?" ³⁴But they remained silent. They had been discussing among themselves on the way who was the greatest. ³⁵Then he sat down, called the Twelve, and said to them, "If anyone wishes to be first, he shall be the last of all and the servant of all." ³⁶Taking a child he placed it in their midst, and putting his arms around it he said to them, ³⁷"Whoever receives one child such as this in my name, receives me; and whoever receives me, receives not me but the One who sent me."
>
> *Another Exorcist*
>
> ³⁸John said to him, "Teacher, we saw someone driving out demons in your name, and we tried to prevent him because he does not follow us." ³⁹Jesus replied, "Do not prevent him. There is no one who performs a mighty deed in my name who can at the same time speak ill of me. ⁴⁰For whoever
>
> *continue*

gressively teaching his disciples how to give up the pursuit of worldly power. He dramatizes Jesus' point by showing him elevate the child (9:36-37).

9:38-40 "Whoever is not against us is for us"

Mark continues in the next episode to stress Jesus' instruction on the yielding of power. He uses the reactions of the disciples as a foil for this teaching. In this scene, the disciples ironically exhibit a worldly sense of competition about the spiritual ministry of exorcism: "Teacher, we saw someone driving out demons in your name, and we tried to prevent him because he does not follow us" (9:38). Mark gives Jesus' response (9:39-40) as further instruction in being one who serves others, not one who seeks to be superior.

Lesson One

is not against us is for us. ⁴¹Anyone who gives you a cup of water to drink because you belong to Christ, amen, I say to you, will surely not lose his reward.

Temptations to Sin

⁴²"Whoever causes one of these little ones who believe [in me] to sin, it would be better for him if a great millstone were put around his neck and he were thrown into the sea. ⁴³If your hand causes you to sin, cut it off. It is better for you to enter into life maimed than with two hands to go into Gehenna, into the unquenchable fire. [⁴⁴] ⁴⁵And if your foot causes you to sin, cut it off. It is better for you to enter into life crippled than with two feet to be thrown into Gehenna. [⁴⁶] ⁴⁷And if your eye causes you to sin, pluck it out. Better for you to enter into the kingdom of God with one eye than with two eyes to be thrown into Gehenna, ⁴⁸where 'their worm does not die, and the fire is not quenched.'

continue

In Mark 9:40, Jesus makes use of a well-known contemporary proverb: **"For whoever is not against us is for us."** In Matthew 12:30 and Luke 11:23, the same proverb appears, but it is stated negatively: "Whoever is not with me is against me." The positively stated proverb in Mark's Gospel may seem strange given this Gospel's clear distinction between "insiders" (the disciples) and "outsiders" (such as the scribes, the crowd, and even Jesus' own family; see Mark 3:20-22; 4:11-12). Jesus' refusal to condemn the man performing exorcisms in his name may point to an apocalyptic theme that looks forward to a future time when the kingdom of God will overwhelm all opposition.

9:41-42 The reward of a cup of water

At this point, the text indicates that Jesus said, "Anyone who gives you a cup of water to drink because you belong to Christ . . . will surely not lose his reward." This saying does not seem to fit in here. Instead, it would seem to fit logically after Jesus' statement "Whoever receives one child such as this in my name, receives me" (9:37). This placement is supported by the fact that the phrase that is translated here as "you belong to Christ" literally reads "because in name you are Christ's."

Mark has been showing how Jesus tried to teach his disciples that being like him means being like a child in powerlessness. And so it follows that whoever receives a child in his name—that is, welcomes the powerless in his name—welcomes him. It would make sense for Jesus to then turn it about and speak of his disciples as the "children" being welcomed by others. Assuming that his disciples will become the powerless he has asked them to be, Jesus goes on to say that anyone who welcomes them in his name (even with as little as a cup of water) will be rewarded.

This rearrangement of verses would also make more sense out of Jesus saying, "Whoever causes one of these little ones who believe [in me] to sin, it would be better for him if a great millstone were put around his neck and he were thrown into the sea" (9:42).

The disciples' complaint about someone outside their group driving out demons in Jesus' name (9:38) would then take on even greater irony. Mark would be showing that instead of getting Jesus' point about powerlessness, the disciples (one more time!) had missed the point and latched on to the phrase "in my name" as the key one. Thus the protest against someone driving out demons in Jesus' name who isn't one of "them."

9:43-48 Being ready to give up everything

The list that follows then makes sense as a continuing part of Jesus' instruction to give up things that most people cling to—even, if necessary, one's very limbs. The terse style in which these teachings are phrased is typical of the Wisdom writings, as is the rhythmical pairings of contrasts: "It is better [to do such and such] than to [do this or that]."

 Gehenna (from the Greek *geena*, derived from the Aramaic *ge-hinnōm*, meaning "valley of the son of Himmon") is the term used in the New Testament for a place of punishment after death, or what we now call "hell." Two possible origins for the use of the term "Gehenna" have been proposed. Scholars have noted that this valley, situated between Jerusalem and the hills to the south and west of the city, was the site of human sacrifices made at a shrine dedicated to the pagan god Moloch (see 2 Kgs 23:10; 2 Chr 28:3; 33:6; Jer 7:31). As the location of such abominable practices, the analogy with a place of torment readily occurred to the minds of the Jewish people. An alternative explanation is that the valley later became a place where trash from Jerusalem was burned, thus suggesting a place of continual fire and punishment.

9:49-50 Being salted

Being salted "with" fire is a bit puzzling, but there is precedent in the Hebrew Bible for linking both elements with purification. We have already noted the passage in Malachi where he speaks of the final messenger of the covenant being like the "refiner's fire" (Mal 3:2). In both Leviticus and Ezekiel, salt is connected with sacrificial offerings that are burned on the altar. Leviticus speaks of the "salt of the covenant": "You shall season all your grain offerings with salt. Do not let the salt of the covenant of your God be lacking from your grain offering" (Lev 2:13). Similarly in Ezekiel, God asks for purifying sacrifices that involve both salt and fire: "When you have completed the purification, you must bring an unblemished young bull and an unblemished ram from the flock and present

> *The Simile of Salt*
>
> ⁴⁹"Everyone will be salted with fire. ⁵⁰Salt is good, but if salt becomes insipid, with what will you restore its flavor? Keep salt in yourselves and you will have peace with one another."
>
> *continue*

them before the LORD. The priests shall throw salt on them and sacrifice them as burnt offerings to the LORD" (Ezek 43:23-24).

Mark has just shown Jesus teaching his disciples to be ready to sacrifice their own bodies, if necessary, in order to be his disciples. It would seem to be in keeping with those demands that he speaks of their purifying themselves with salt and fire. When Mark shows Jesus saying in conclusion, "Keep salt in yourselves" (9:50), he would seem to be referring to both "the salt of the covenant" and the fire of self-sacrifice that he himself will model.

Summary of chapter 9

The chapter shifts the readers' focus and makes plain things hidden before. The scene of Jesus' transfiguration begins this shift by revealing the inner and future glory of both Jesus and his disciples. Mark designs this revelation to come before the narrative of Jesus' shameful death so that it will overshadow it. It points to Jesus' resurrection.

At the same time, the chapter is unified by a new perspective on power. The transfiguration reveals a splendor that will transform the ignominy of rejection and death. The casting out of demons is revealed to be not a matter of super power but of simple faith and prayer. The servant and the child are held up as the greatest. God's power is declared to be inclusive and not restricted to an inner circle. Jesus teaches that it is better to be crippled for God than to remain strong and not be for him. In conclusion, Jesus teaches that the "fire" of sacrificing oneself may be the "salt" needed to season the kingdom.

Lesson One

CHAPTER 10

Marriage and Divorce

¹He set out from there and went into the district of Judea [and] across the Jordan. Again crowds gathered around him and, as was his custom, he again taught them. ²The Pharisees approached and asked, "Is it lawful for a husband to divorce his wife?" They were testing him. ³He said to them in reply, "What did Moses command you?" ⁴They replied, "Moses permitted him to write a bill of divorce and dismiss her." ⁵But Jesus told them, "Because of the hardness of your hearts he wrote you this commandment. ⁶But from the beginning of creation, 'God made them male and female. ⁷For this reason a man shall leave his father and mother [and be joined to his wife], ⁸and the two shall become one flesh.' So they are no longer two but one flesh. ⁹Therefore what God has joined together, no human being must separate."
¹⁰In the house the disciples again questioned him about this. ¹¹He said to them, "Whoever divorces his wife and marries another commits adultery against her; ¹²and if she divorces her husband and marries another, she commits adultery."

continue

RETURN TO THE BEGINNING

Mark 10:1-52

10:1-12 "From the beginning of creation"

This discussion of divorce is usually treated apart from Mark's whole Gospel. Abstracted in that way from its context, Jesus' words on marriage appear to be stricter and less flexible than the present teachings of the church. But if the passage is read in its whole setting, a different sense emerges. In the preceding chapter, Mark has shown Jesus elevating a child (9:36-37), and in the passage that immediately follows this one, Mark shows Jesus saying, "Whoever does not accept the kingdom of God like a child will not enter it" (10:15). In fact, the whole of chapter 10 (as we are about to show) is focused on how to live with childlike simplicity. In this passage on marriage, Mark sets up this focus by giving Jesus' reference to "the beginning of creation" (10:6). "The beginning of creation" is the frame for the whole chapter.

In Jewish thought about the end time (that is, the projected moment when, it was believed, the will of God would entirely prevail), there were two distinct strains of thought. One view held that God would prevail as judge, destroying the wicked and preserving the good. The other view held that God would act as a healer and redeemer, restoring his people and leading them back, as it were, to their original state in the Garden of Eden. In the Prophets, one hears a lot about God's judgment on Israel; it is associated with the destruction of Jerusalem and especially the Temple, as well as the defeat and captivity of Israel. In the prophetic imagination, however, God's final judgments are rendered only on the nations that besiege and corrupt Israel. God's judgments on Israel itself are temporary. The prophet always envisions that in the end time God will restore his people to virtue, his Temple to its original state as a house of prayer, and the land to its original condition of abundance and fertility.

In the Wisdom writings, the prevailing imagery is of the Garden. The Psalms sing of how God created human beings for glory ("You have made him little less than a god," Ps 8:6); how God preserves his people from destruction (They shall be "like a tree / planted near streams of water, / that yields its fruit in season," Ps 1:3); how God restores them after a time of wandering or distress ("to still waters he leads me; / he restores my soul," Ps 23:2-3). The Song of Songs imagines the Garden as the setting for the love affair between God and humanity. The book of Sirach associates the Garden imagery of the Song with the feminine figure of God's Wisdom. The book of Job, for all its tragic disaster, concludes with a reminder of the majesty of creation, the restoration of Job, and a new beginning. The cynical preacher in Ecclesiastes changes from finding that "all is vanity" to a new trust in God's power to create. The author of the Wisdom of Solomon takes the idea of restoration a step further by perceiving that Wisdom in the human soul is a reflection of God's immortality. In all of these writings, while God's judgment on evil is certainly assumed and articulated, there is also a sense that the true human destiny is to return to the original Garden. To say that Mark shows "the beginning of creation" to be the framework for Jesus' teachings is to imply his reference to this whole tradition.

It is this tradition that Mark shows at work here when he tells us that Jesus quoted Genesis 2:24 (10:7-8) and contrasted its ideal of married oneness with the bill of divorce that Moses allowed as a concession to the "hardness of your hearts" (10:5).

Mark has used the phrase "hardness of heart" twice before—once to describe the Pharisees when they begrudge Jesus' healing on the Sabbath (3:5) and again to describe the disciples when they fail to understand the miracle of the loaves (6:52). In all three instances, the phrase does not indicate the commitment of a sin but the failure to measure up to an ideal standard. So here, we may infer, Mark shows Jesus using this phrase to indicate a falling away from the ideal human state.

10:13-16 Children as the ideal members of God's kingdom

In describing Jesus' blessing of the children here, Mark echoes and develops the scene in the previous chapter (9:36-37) where Jesus embraces a child and says, "Whoever receives one child such as this in my name, receives me." As we noted before, in that context Jesus seems to be teaching his disciples the value of powerlessness. This idea seems to be confirmed and clarified by what Mark shows Jesus saying here: "Whoever does not accept the kingdom of God like a child will not enter it" (10:15).

> ### Blessing of the Children
>
> [13] And people were bringing children to him that he might touch them, but the disciples rebuked them. [14] When Jesus saw this he became indignant and said to them, "Let the children come to me; do not prevent them, for the kingdom of God belongs to such as these. [15] Amen, I say to you, whoever does not accept the kingdom of God like a child will not enter it." [16] Then he embraced them and blessed them, placing his hands on them.
>
> *continue*

It has been suggested that Jesus **embracing and blessing the children** resembles the Jewish tradition of having children brought to the scribes/elders to be blessed on the Day of Atonement. It is unclear, however, whether this custom was actually practiced in Jesus' time. Another possible model for Jesus' actions is the bestowal of parental blessings on children found in the Old Testament (Gen 9:26-27; 27:1-40; 28:1-4; 48:8-17). Regardless of any parallels, what is most striking about Jesus' action is the way he elevates children as a model of discipleship. In the Old Testament, children are most often portrayed as dependents requiring instruction and discipline (e.g., Prov 5:7; 13:24; 29:17), a common attitude in ancient Mediterranean cultures. Jesus' acceptance and elevation of children as a model for adult behavior continues the prominent Markan reversal theme in which Jesus seeks out the poor rather than the rich, sinners rather than the righteous, and the sick rather than the healthy.

The Rich Man

[17] As he was setting out on a journey, a man ran up, knelt down before him, and asked him, "Good teacher, what must I do to inherit eternal life?" [18] Jesus answered him, "Why do you call me good? No one is good but God alone. [19] You know the commandments: 'You shall not kill; you shall not commit adultery; you shall not steal; you shall not bear false witness; you shall not defraud; honor your father and your mother.'" [20] He replied and said to him, "Teacher, all of these I have observed from my youth." [21] Jesus, looking at him, loved him and said to him, "You are lacking in one thing. Go, sell what you have, and give to [the] poor and you will have treasure in heaven; then come, follow me." [22] At that statement his face fell, and he went away sad, for he had many possessions.

[23] Jesus looked around and said to his disciples, "How hard it is for those who have wealth to enter the kingdom of God!" [24] The disciples were

continue

10:17-31 The poor as ideal members of the kingdom

The story of the rich man who cannot follow Jesus is of a piece with this emphasis. The man affirms that he has kept the Ten Commandments from his youth (10:20), a declaration that indicates his essential goodness. And Mark goes on to say that Jesus "loved him" (10:21). Nonetheless, Mark shows Jesus asking more of him: "You are lacking in one thing. Go, sell what you have, and give to [the] poor, and you will have treasure in heaven; then come, follow me" (10:21).

Just as in the teachings about being faithful in marriage and about becoming childlike, Mark shows Jesus holding up an ideal. It is an ideal that is in keeping with Jesus' other teachings on detachment. Just as Mark shows Jesus teaching his disciples to detach themselves from power by becoming like children, so here he shows Jesus teaching them to detach themselves from possessions. By showing that despite his goodness, this rich man cannot follow Jesus' instruction (10:22), Mark indicates that Jesus is setting up a norm for holiness that demands far more than the conventional one. In the discussion with the disciples that follows (10:23-33), Mark further dramatizes the unconventionality of Jesus' request.

Mark does this by setting up a dialogue between Jesus and his disciples, in which Jesus repeatedly stresses "how hard" it is for the wealthy to enter God's kingdom, while the disciples repeatedly express their astonishment at what he is saying (10:23-26). (Jesus' statement that "It is easier for a camel . . . " has a rabbinic parallel—"It is easier for an elephant . . ."—and so should not be seen as a special riddle of Jesus, but simply as an exaggeration typical of first-century Jewish teachers.)

The climax of this dialogue occurs when the disciples ask, "Then who can be saved?" and Jesus responds, "For human beings it is impossible, but not for God. All things are possible for God" (10:26-27). In this pithy exchange, Mark shows that Jesus was asking his followers to commit themselves to a way of living that could not be accomplished without God's grace. He was shifting the burden from their need for self-sufficiency to their need for total dependence on God. This acknowledgment of total dependence is, of course, the ultimate poverty, the ultimate detachment.

 Many interpretations have been offered to explain the analogy of the **camel passing through the eye of a needle** (Mark 10:25), including identifying the "eye of a needle" with a particularly narrow gate that supposedly led into Jerusalem. But there are good reasons to interpret this verse as it is normally understood. The camel was the largest land animal in Palestine, and there are examples both in Scripture and elsewhere that use the camel in contrast with a much smaller animal to indicate two extremes. In Matthew 23:24, for example, the camel and the gnat are contrasted.

In underscoring the obstacle that wealth can be for one who seeks to follow Jesus, the camel (which in Isaiah 60:6 is pictured as being weighted down with "gold and frankincense") serves as an apt symbol of those who are burdened with riches. As St. Jerome points out in his commentary on Matthew's Gospel, it is only once the heavy burden of wealth is offloaded and discarded that the camel/rich man can enter the heavenly city.

10:28-31, 35-45 The disciples' failure to understand

In the exchange that follows between Peter and Jesus (10:28-31), Mark shows how little Peter has understood. Peter's response to Jesus' request for this total detachment is to protest that he has already accomplished it: "We have given up everything and followed you" (10:28). Jesus' reply is indirect, not directly disagreeing, and indeed promising rewards in this life and "eternal life in the age to come" (10:30). Yet among his promises, Mark shows Jesus slipping in "persecutions," a reminder that following Jesus will involve following him in the way of suffering. Jesus' final assertion, "Many that are first will be last and [the] last will be first" (10:31), is also a reminder of the paradox of the cross.

Mark particularly dramatizes the disciples' failure to grasp that final lesson when he shows James and John asking to be first in glory (10:37). Mark introduces this ironic question by showing James and John talking to Jesus as if he were their servant: "We want you to do for us whatever we ask of you" (10:35). And he shows Jesus accepting this role: "What do you wish [me] to do for you?" (10:36). In the exchange that follows between Jesus and his disciples, Mark shows the extent of the gap in the disciples' understanding.

The reply that Mark shows Jesus giving here is central to Mark's interpretation of Jesus' theology. First, he shows Jesus speaking cryptically of his "cup" and his "baptism" (10:38-39). In the Psalms, "cup" is figuratively linked

---

amazed at his words. So Jesus again said to them in reply, "Children, how hard it is to enter the kingdom of God! ²⁵It is easier for a camel to pass through [the] eye of [a] needle than for one who is rich to enter the kingdom of God." ²⁶They were exceedingly astonished and said among themselves, "Then who can be saved?" ²⁷Jesus looked at them and said, "For human beings it is impossible, but not for God. All things are possible for God." ²⁸Peter began to say to him, "We have given up everything and followed you." ²⁹Jesus said, "Amen, I say to you, there is no one who has given up house or brothers or sisters or mother or father or children or lands for my sake and for the sake of the gospel ³⁰who will not receive a hundred times more now in this present age: houses and brothers and sisters and mothers and children and lands, with persecutions, and eternal life in the age to come. ³¹But many that are first will be last, and [the] last will be first."

continue

---

to one's inheritance or destiny ("Lord, my allotted portion and my cup," Ps 16:5) and to salvation ("I will raise the cup of salvation / and call on the name of the Lord," Ps 116:13). "Baptism" is not a word used in the Hebrew Bible, although the ritual immersion that it connotes was part of Judaism and signified (as it does in Mark) a change of heart. These words take on additional meaning here. Jesus' use of the word "cup" suggests the cup of wine that he will later designate as the cup of his blood (14:23-24), and his use of the word "baptism" also suggests a link with his death.

Paul emphasizes this link when he asks, "Are you unaware that we who were baptized into Christ Jesus were baptized into his death?" (Rom 6:3). When Mark shows James and John being quick to accept this "cup" and "baptism" (10:39), he indicates that they are not making these same connections with death. Mark confirms this lack of awareness when he shows Jesus saying, "You do not know what you are asking" (10:38).

Lesson One

God - "ancient of days" - book of Daniel

3rd prediction
a sign to followers

The Third Prediction of the Passion

³²They were on the way, going up to Jerusalem, and Jesus went ahead of them. They were amazed, and those who followed were afraid. Taking the Twelve aside again, he began to tell them what was going to happen to him. ³³"Behold, we are going up to Jerusalem, and the Son of Man will be handed over to the chief priests and the scribes, and they will condemn him to death and hand him over to the Gentiles ³⁴who will mock him, spit upon him, scourge him, and put him to death, but after three days he will rise."

Ambition of James and John

don't get it

³⁵Then James and John, the sons of Zebedee, came to him and said to him, "Teacher, we want you to do for us whatever we ask of you." ³⁶He replied, "What do you wish [me] to do for you?" ³⁷They answered him, "Grant that in your glory we may sit one at your right and the other at your left." ³⁸Jesus said to them, "You do not know what you are asking. Can you drink the cup that I drink or be baptized with the baptism with which I am baptized?" ³⁹They said to him, "We can." Jesus said to them, "The cup that I drink, you will drink, and with the baptism with which I am baptized, you will be baptized; ⁴⁰but to sit at my right or at my left is not mine to give but is for those for whom it has been prepared." ⁴¹When the ten heard this, they

continue

Jesus telling them how they should act: "Whoever wishes to be first among you will be the slave of all" (10:44). Last, and most important, Mark shows Jesus explaining that by so doing, they will truly be his disciples, because he came expressly "not to be served but to serve" (10:45). Beyond that, Mark suggests by his final phrase that Jesus has come to offer the ultimate service of giving up his life for the sake of others.

The phrase "to give his life as a ransom for many" is a reference to Isaiah 53:11, where God is speaking about his chosen servant, who will offer his life as an atoning sacrifice for the sins of others. This is the last of those passages in Isaiah known as the "Songs of the Suffering Servant." In Isaiah, the Servant is identified as Israel—God's righteous servant among the nations, who is put to death by the kings of the world because they do not understand Israel's God-blessed nature or mission. By quoting this phrase as part of Jesus' self-understanding, Mark suggests that Jesus can be understood through the same lens: he is God's righteous servant; he will be put to death by Gentile powers that fail to understand him; he will offer his life as an atonement for the sins of others; he will ultimately be exalted by God.

 Jesus made it very clear to his disciples that their importance arises not out of their greatness but out of their **service**, and that their service must flow out of their humility—their willingness to stand beside rather than lord prestige or power over someone.

By giving the ironic request of James and John, Mark sets the stage for a fuller illumination of Jesus' teaching on worldly power (10:42-45). He shows Jesus here giving his disciples the plainest explanation of what he is about. Mark first shows Jesus distancing himself from the worldly, Gentile conventions of power, in which "those who are recognized as rulers . . . lord it over" others and "make their authority . . . felt" (10:42). Then Mark shows Jesus directly rejecting this approach: "It shall not be so among you" (10:43). Next, he shows

10:32-34 Jesus' third prediction of his death

Mark interweaves Jesus' third prediction of his own suffering in between the episodes that show the failure of Peter, James, and John to understand that as Jesus' disciples they have been called to dispossession, service, and death. It is a structure we have seen Mark use before. Just as he placed the story of John the Baptist's

Peace be upon him,

death in the middle of the first sending forth of the disciples (6:14-29), so here he places the prediction of Jesus' death between the episode showing Peter's confidence that he has already given up everything and the episode of the request of James and John for glory.

Mark, moreover, shows Jesus being explicit here in a way that he never has been before. In the first prediction, Mark quotes Jesus speaking vaguely about how he must "suffer greatly . . . be rejected . . . be killed, . . . and rise after three days" (8:31). In the second prediction, Mark shows Jesus adding the element of betrayal, but generalizing everything else: "The Son of Man is to be handed over to [human beings] and they will kill him, and three days after his death he will rise" (9:31). Here Mark shows Jesus speaking specifically about "going up to Jerusalem" and about how he will be handed over "to the chief priests and the scribes," who will, in turn, "hand him over to the Gentiles, who will mock him, spit upon him, scourge him, and put him to death" (10:33-34). If we look at these three predictions as one of Mark's triads, the middle prediction is key, indicating that "human beings" in general are responsible for Jesus' death. But within Mark's narrative, the concreteness of the third prediction is Mark's way of sharpening the irony of the disciples' lack of understanding.

10:46-52 The symbolic cure of the blind man

This is another miracle of healing that has a symbolic and summarizing function. In 8:22-26, Mark shows Jesus healing a blind man in two stages. We noted that the miracle echoes the earlier healing of the deaf-mute (7:33) and completes Jesus' relationship to the passage in Isaiah where "the ears of the deaf" are "opened" and "the eyes of the blind shall see" (Isa 35:5-6). At the same time, the two-stage process alerts the reader to the meaning behind Mark's doublet structure. In the next miraculous healing (9:14-29), a deaf-mute is cured again. In describing this cure, Mark incorporates a number of elements that have been part of several earlier miracles, so that this miracle

became indignant at James and John. ⁴²Jesus summoned them and said to them, "You know that those who are recognized as rulers over the Gentiles lord it over them, and their great ones make their authority over them felt. ⁴³But it shall not be so among you. Rather, whoever wishes to be great among you will be your servant; ⁴⁴whoever wishes to be first among you will be the slave of all. ⁴⁵For the Son of Man did not come to be served but to serve and to give his life as a ransom for many."

The Blind Bartimaeus

⁴⁶They came to Jericho. And as he was leaving Jericho with his disciples and a sizable crowd, Bartimaeus, a blind man, the son of Timaeus, sat by the roadside begging. ⁴⁷On hearing that it was Jesus of Nazareth, he began to cry out and say, "Jesus, son of David, have pity on me." ⁴⁸And many rebuked him, telling him to be silent. But he kept calling out all the more, "Son of David, have pity on me." ⁴⁹Jesus stopped and said, "Call him." So they called the blind man, saying to him, "Take courage; get up, he is calling you." ⁵⁰He threw aside his cloak, sprang up, and came to Jesus. ⁵¹Jesus said to him in reply, "What do you want me to do for you?" The blind man replied to him, "Master, I want to see." ⁵²Jesus told him, "Go your way; your faith has saved you." Immediately he received his sight and followed him on the way.

incorporates what has gone before. In the same way, this cure of the blind man Bartimaeus appears to be a doublet, and more than a doublet, of the cure of the blind man in chapter 8.

Within the immediate narrative, the story of the blind beggar reverses that of the rich man. The rich man could not become a disciple of Jesus because of his many possessions. The beggar has no possessions except his cloak, and he immediately casts that away to come to Jesus (10:50). In the end, the blind man not only receives his sight from Jesus but "followed him on the way" (10:52).

Beyond that, the name Bartimaeus literally means "son of the unclean" in Hebrew, so the name alone has a summarizing function. In the first part of his Gospel, Mark has shown Jesus to be in constant association with "the unclean" of his society—demoniacs, lepers, tax collectors, sinners, a woman with a flow of blood, and a dead body. When Mark shows Jesus healing someone who is named "son of the unclean," he is reminding his readers of them all.

Mark also shows this blind man to have other distinctive characteristics. Unlike the first blind man, who was brought to Jesus by others, this one calls out to him (10:47). Mark shows him addressing Jesus, moreover, as "son of David," a title that indicates he recognizes Jesus as God's chosen agent. There is a certain irony, therefore, in his request to see (10:51), because he seems to already be seeing more than many sighted folk around him. Mark shows Jesus confirming this when he says, "Go your way; your faith has saved you" (10:52). In showing Jesus' cure of Bartimaeus, Mark sums up how Jesus can heal and restore all "the unclean" who have faith in God's outreach to them.

In this summarizing incident, Mark echoes certain words from the first part of his Gospel. When he says that the blind man "began to cry out" (10:47), we hear an echo of the unclean spirit in chapter 5, who also cried out to Jesus (5:5). The intent, however, is the reverse: the unclean spirit wanted Jesus to go away; the blind man wants him to come near. When Mark describes the disciples' telling the blind man to "take courage" (10:49), he uses the same word that he shows Jesus saying to his frightened disciples in chapter 6 (6:50). But again there is a difference: the disciples remain fearful; the blind man seems to need no encouragement, for he springs up and goes to Jesus (10:50). The phrase that is translated here as "get up" (10:49) is in fact *"rise* up"* and thus an echo of Jesus' words to the dead child in chapter 5 (5:41). Jesus' final words to the blind man, "Your faith has saved you" (10:52), repeats his final words to the woman healed of her flow of blood (5:34). In ending this narrative, Mark says that "*Straightway** [translated here as 'immediately'] he received his sight" (10:52). In short, there are enough key words in this short episode to suggest that Mark is loading it with particular significance. It is as though Mark wanted to suggest the possibility for all people—whether blinded by demons or by fear or by "uncleanness" or even by death—to be restored, to have their lives "made straight" again.

Summary of chapter 10

In this chapter, Mark shows Jesus pointing to "the beginning of creation" as revealing God's intended destiny for human beings, and trying to teach his disciples how to return to that state of original simplicity. Mark shows Jesus doing this in several ways. First, he shows Jesus referring to the beginning unity between man and woman as the norm for human relationships. Then he shows him holding up children as models of the detachment from power necessary to enter the kingdom. Next, through setting up a dialogue between Jesus and a rich man, he shows Jesus teaching his disciples that they need to divest themselves of all possessions and learn to depend totally upon God's providence. Mark then indicates the disciples' failure to understand these teachings by showing parallel episodes that involve the three key disciples—Peter first, then James and John. Mark sharpens the irony of the disciples' obtuseness by placing in between these episodes Jesus' third and most explicit prediction of his own suffering and death.

In conclusion, Mark shows the healing of a blind beggar who, out of his powerlessness and poverty, is ready to become a disciple of Jesus. He is a beggar whose name means "son of the unclean" and whose cure, as Mark constructs the story, echoes and summarizes many of Jesus' earlier miracles. When Mark ends this narrative by saying, "Straightway* he received his sight and followed him on the way" (10:52), he affirms the potential for every human being to follow Jesus' way of return to the beginning.

Lesson One

EXPLORING LESSON ONE

1. When have you witnessed others demonstrating the value of service over striving to achieve public importance (9:33-37)? What stands out in their example?

2. What "mighty deeds" performed in unexpected places or by unexpected people (9:38-41) have helped reveal Christ to you?

3. How is salt shown to be of importance in the Old Testament (9:49-50)? (See Lev 2:13; 2 Kgs 2:20-22; 2 Chr 13:5; Ezek 43:23-24.)

4. a) Describe some of the difficulties married people experience that put stress on permanent marriage commitments (10:1-2).

   b) How can we as individuals and parish communities support families who are struggling today?

Lesson One

5. What characteristics of childhood do you think make children examples of how we are to accept the kingdom of God (10:15)?

6. a) What does the request of James and John—and Jesus' reply to them—teach you about ambition (10:35-45)? (See Matt 18:1-5; Jas 4:1-3.)

    b) What does Scripture teach us is deserving of our ambition? (See 1 Cor 12:31; Phil 3:14.)

7. Why is "the cup" an important symbol when Jesus asks James and John if they can drink from the cup that Jesus drinks from (10:35-45)? (See Mark 14:24; Ps 16:5; 116:13; Ezek 23:33.)

8. In what significant ways does the healing of Bartimaeus (10:46-52) differ from the healing of the blind man in Mark 8:22-26?

CLOSING PRAYER

Prayer

Jesus, looking at him, loved him and said to him, "You are lacking in one thing. Go, sell what you have, and give to [the] poor and you will have treasure in heaven; then come, follow me."

(Mark 10:21)

Jesus, we know you love us and order all things for our benefit. Help us to let go of anything that stands in the way of our returning your love and being your disciples. Today we especially ask you to free us from . . .

LESSON TWO

Mark 11–12

Begin your personal study and group discussion with a simple and sincere prayer such as:

Prayer

> Lord Jesus, as we read this Gospel, may we hear your words and meditate on your life with open hearts and alert minds. May our time of study and sharing strengthen our faith in you, the source of all truth and wisdom.

Read the Bible text of Mark 11–12 found in the outside columns of pages 30–41, highlighting what stands out to you.

Read the accompanying commentary to add to your understanding.

Respond to the questions on pages 42–43, Exploring Lesson Two.

The Closing Prayer on page 44 is for your personal use and may be used at the end of group discussion.

Lesson Two radical – radis = root

CHAPTER 11

The Entry into Jerusalem

¹When they drew near to Jerusalem, to Bethphage and Bethany at the Mount of Olives, he sent two of his disciples ²and said to them, "Go into the village opposite you, and immediately on entering it, you will find a colt tethered on which no one has ever sat. Untie it and bring it here. ³If anyone should say to you, 'Why are you doing this?' reply, 'The Master has need of it and will send it back here at once.'" ⁴So they went off and found a colt tethered at a gate outside on the street, and they untied it. ⁵Some of the bystanders said to them, "What are you doing, untying the colt?" ⁶They answered them just as Jesus had told them to, and they permitted them to do it. ⁷So they brought the colt to Jesus and put their cloaks over it. And he sat on it. ⁸Many people spread their cloaks on the road, and others spread leafy branches that they had cut from the fields. ⁹Those preceding him as well as those following kept crying out:

"Hosanna!
  Blessed is he who comes in the name of
    the Lord!
¹⁰Blessed is the kingdom of our father
    David that is to come!
  Hosanna in the highest!"

¹¹He entered Jerusalem and went into the temple area. He looked around at everything and, since it was already late, went out to Bethany with the Twelve.

continue

JESUS AND THE TEMPLE AUTHORITIES—NEW UNDERSTANDINGS OF POWER

Mark 11:1-37

11:1-11 Jesus' entry into Jerusalem

In this opening scene, Mark picks up on the cure of the blind beggar by showing the people spreading their cloaks on the ground (11:8) and crying out, "Blessed is the kingdom of our father David that is to come!" (11:10). Their cry also echoes the first proclamation of John the Baptist, "One mightier than I is coming after me" (1:7). Yet Mark modifies the impression of triumphant entry by describing Jesus riding on a colt.

In the whole next section of his Gospel, Mark shows Jesus acting out the new understandings of power he has been trying to teach his disciples. Mark also shifts his style, showing Jesus, like many of the prophets, engaged in symbolic or parabolic action. To begin with, by showing the lengths to which Jesus goes to ride into Jerusalem on a colt (11:1-7), Mark calls attention to the relationship between Jesus and the words of Zechariah:

Behold: your king is coming to you,
  a just savior is he,
Humble, and riding on a donkey,
  on a colt, the foal of a donkey (9:9).

In Zechariah, the predicted king is unknown and mysterious. One of the most striking details in Zechariah's description is this picture of him entering Jerusalem on "the foal of a donkey." The choice of the donkey not only suggests humility but peacemaking; in ancient times war was associated with the horse. Zechariah goes on to say that this king will "banish

". . . the horse from Jerusalem" along with "the warrior's bow," and "he will proclaim peace to the nations" (9:10). The passages that follow in Zechariah are complex, but essentially the coming of this peace-loving king begins the restoration of Jerusalem.

At the same time, Mark echoes, through the images of the people spreading "leafy branches" and crying out "Hosanna" (11:8), the description in the first book of Maccabees of Simon Maccabeus entering Jerusalem with praise and palm branches to take back the Temple from the Greek tyrant Antiochus IV (1 Macc 13:47-52).

We have spoken before about how different foreign conquerors of Jerusalem tried to take over the Temple and weaken Jewish religion. One of the most despised was Antiochus IV, a Greek ruler of Palestine two centuries before the time of Jesus. He tried to virtually eradicate Jewish faith in a number of ways. He ordered the substitution of the Greek constitution for the Hebrew Bible. He forbade circumcision, and if mothers violated his edict, he killed their babies and hung the dead infants around their necks. He erected a statue of himself in the Temple. This statue of Antiochus is referred to in Daniel 12:11 as "the desolating abomination" (a phrase that is used by Mark, as we will see, in chapter 13).

It was the last straw for the Jewish people. They rose up in revolt, led by the seven Maccabee brothers. Their success in restoring the Temple is still celebrated in the annual feast of Hanukkah. The first book of Maccabees records that Simon Maccabeus cleansed the Temple of Antiochus's statue and all his other profanities (1 Macc 13:50b).

By using language that would remind his readers of both Zechariah's peace-loving king and of Simon Maccabeus, Mark offers a complex picture of Jesus. Both scriptural passages converge in showing someone who took action to restore the Temple to its original state as a place of worship. Yet there is a tension between the two. As Mark develops his portrait of Jesus' relationship to the Temple, he also continues to show this tension.

Jesus Curses a Fig Tree

¹²The next day as they were leaving Bethany he was hungry. ¹³Seeing from a distance a fig tree in leaf, he went over to see if he could find anything on it. When he reached it he found nothing but leaves; it was not the time for figs. ¹⁴And he said to it in reply, "May no one ever eat of your fruit again!" And his disciples heard it.

Cleansing of the Temple

¹⁵They came to Jerusalem, and on entering the temple area he began to drive out those selling and buying there. He overturned the tables of the money changers and the seats of those who were selling doves. ¹⁶He did not permit anyone to carry

continue

The shouts of praise that greet Jesus on his triumphal entry into Jerusalem (11:10) have been incorporated by the church into the liturgy of the Mass, where they are proclaimed by the entire congregation immediately before the beginning of the eucharistic prayer. The word **Hosanna** in its Aramaic form literally means "Save, we pray." Much of the language describing this scene echoes Psalm 118, while the general air of rejoicing and the spreading of "leafy branches . . . cut from the fields" (11:8) are reminiscent of the ritual for celebrating the Jewish feast of Tabernacles (see Lev 23:40).

11:15-19 Jesus' "cleansing of the Temple"

It is interesting to note that the phrase "cleansing of the Temple" is not used by Mark. The caption is an editor's choice; one can only speculate that the editor was thinking of the book of Maccabees. In any event, the episode that follows, like the opening one of the chapter, is constructed out of interweaving echoes

Lesson Two

> anything through the temple area. ¹⁷Then he taught them saying, "Is it not written:
>
> > 'My house shall be called a house of prayer
> > for all peoples'?
> > But you have made it a den of thieves."
>
> ¹⁸The chief priests and the scribes came to hear of it and were seeking a way to put him to death, yet they feared him because the whole crowd was astonished at his teaching. ¹⁹When evening came, they went out of the city.
>
> **The Withered Fig Tree**
>
> ²⁰Early in the morning, as they were walking along, they saw the fig tree withered to its roots. ²¹Peter remembered and said to him, "Rabbi, look! The fig tree that you cursed has withered."
>
> *continue*

of the Hebrew Scripture. The key echoes occur in what Mark shows Jesus teaching:

> My house shall be called a house of prayer for
> all peoples.
> > But you have made it a den of thieves
> > (11:17).

The first line here is a direct quote from Isaiah 56:7, while the second comes from Jeremiah 7:11. The passage in Isaiah is expressing his vision of a time when God will welcome foreigners to the Temple:

> All who keep the sabbath without profaning it
> and hold fast to my covenant,
> Them I will bring to my holy mountain
> and make them joyful in my house of prayer
> (56:6-7).

The passage from Jeremiah comes from what is known as his "Temple sermon." It is a long passage in which the prophet expresses God's anger at the people's breaking of the covenant and his demand for their moral reform:

> Do not put your trust in these deceptive words: "The temple of the Lord! The temple of the Lord! The temple of the Lord!" Only if you thoroughly reform your ways and your deeds; if each of you deals justly with your neighbor; if you no longer oppress the alien, the orphan, and the widow; if you no longer shed innocent blood in this place or follow after other gods to your own harm, only then will I let you continue to dwell in this place. . . .
>
> Do you think you can steal and murder, commit adultery and perjury, sacrifice to Baal, follow other gods that you do not know, and then come and stand in my presence in this house, which bears my name, and say: "We are safe! We can commit all these abominations again!"? Has this house which bears my name become in your eyes a den of thieves? (Jer 7:4-7, 9-11).

In interweaving these two passages, Mark is juxtaposing two very different strands in biblical tradition. The passage from Jeremiah expresses a warning about being corrupted by foreigners who will not only encourage burning incense to a foreign god but will also foster the weakening of covenant commitments. The passage from Isaiah expresses the vision of a time when foreigners will want to join Israel in worshiping the one God, and all people will be joyfully one in prayer. By showing Jesus quoting both these passages at once—indeed, even making one sentence out of them—Mark again suggests a tension and a complexity in Jesus' attitude toward the Temple. On the one hand, the quotation from Jeremiah places him in the tradition of the reforming prophets seeking to purify Temple worship of foreign influences. On the other hand, the quotation from Isaiah places him in the tradition of the visionary prophets seeking to bring all people together by welcoming foreigners into God's house.

When Mark shows Jesus driving out "those selling and buying" and overturning "the tables of the money changers" and not permitting "anyone to carry anything through the temple area" (11:15-16), these actions must be understood in the context of these prophetic traditions. In the light of these traditions, it does not make sense to assume (as many have) that Mark was indicating that Jesus' actions were hostile to the Temple per se. Nor does it make sense to assume that Jesus was expressing anger at a Temple system that allowed money on the premises.

Some historical background sheds light on the latter. It was customary for Jews to purchase an animal to sacrifice in the Temple, and while they ordinarily used Roman coins in their business transactions, they did not think that appropriate for sacred matters. The Temple authorities accordingly allowed them to exchange their Roman coin for a special Temple coin, which could then be used for their sacrifice. Such a system was no more scandalous than the money collections taken up today in Christian churches.

The prophetic tradition, exemplified in Jeremiah, of criticizing the gap between Temple worship and moral behavior, explains Mark's intent in showing Jesus' anger at the "buyers and sellers" in the Temple. Mark is not suggesting that Jesus was reacting to the custom of money exchange or that he wanted to overturn the whole Temple. Rather, Mark is suggesting that, like reforming prophets before him, Jesus wanted to purify the Temple of the foreign influences that had commercialized it. Under Rome, this commercialization had taken the specific form of turning the priesthood into a political job. The high priests were appointed by Rome and collaborated with the Romans. Some who might have been committed to the Temple became committed instead to collecting taxes for the empire. It is this overall picture of Jewish faith corrupted by venal interests that Mark conveys here. It is opposition to this corruption of faith that Mark shows Jesus symbolizing by overturning the tables of the money changers.

Mark's perspective is signaled by the scriptural contexts he provides for Jesus' action: Maccabees, Jeremiah, Isaiah. By alluding to Maccabees, Mark indicates that Jesus is "cleansing the Temple," as Simon Maccabeus did, from the idolatrous perversion of Jewish worship caused by foreign occupiers. By quoting Jeremiah, Mark indicates that Jesus is angry, as Jeremiah was, at the weakening of

> [22]Jesus said to them in reply, "Have faith in God. [23]Amen, I say to you, whoever says to this mountain, 'Be lifted up and thrown into the sea,' and does not doubt in his heart but believes that what he says will happen, it shall be done for him. [24]Therefore I tell you, all that you ask for in prayer, believe that you will receive it and it shall be yours. [25]When you stand to pray, forgive anyone against whom you have a grievance, so that your heavenly Father may in turn forgive you your transgressions." [26]
>
> **The Authority of Jesus Questioned**
>
> [27]They returned once more to Jerusalem. As he was walking in the temple area, the chief priests, the scribes, and the elders approached him [28]and said to him, "By what authority are you
>
> *continue*

the covenant. But by also quoting Isaiah, Mark indicates that Jesus has a countering prophetic vision of a time when foreigners would be included in the covenant.

11:12-14, 20-28 The fig tree

Two episodes involving the fig tree enclose the symbolic action in the Temple. It is a typical Markan structure and indicates a relationship between the scenes. To understand them, it helps to know the symbolism of the fig tree in first-century Jewish thought. First of all, the fig tree was considered to be the tree that was forbidden in the Garden of Eden. (It is an interpretation that makes sense when you consider that fig trees are indigenous to that part of the world, and that Genesis 3:7 says that Adam and Eve sewed together fig leaves for their first form of clothing.) Second, a fig tree in bloom was considered to be a sign of the end time, of God's final kingdom.

It is also important to consider that Jesus' curse of the fig tree is related to God's curse of the ground when Adam and Eve leave the Garden (Gen 3:17). In Genesis, God tells Adam and

> doing these things? Or who gave you this authority to do them?" ²⁹Jesus said to them, "I shall ask you one question. Answer me, and I will tell you by what authority I do these things. ³⁰Was John's baptism of heavenly or of human origin? Answer me." ³¹They discussed this among themselves and said, "If we say, 'Of heavenly origin,' he will say, '[Then] why did you not believe him?' ³²But shall we say, 'Of human origin'?"—they feared the crowd, for they all thought John really was a prophet. ³³So they said to Jesus in reply, "We do not know." Then Jesus said to them, "Neither shall I tell you by what authority I do these things."
>
> *continue*

Eve that the ground will only bring forth "thorns and thistles" for them (Gen 3:18). In Isaiah, however, this curse is explicitly reversed, and God says he will make the cypress grow instead of the thornbush, and the myrtle instead of nettles (Isa 55:13). Jesus' curse is often translated (as it is here) in such a way that it seems irreversible. But some scholars have suggested that the phrasing is more accurately rendered, "May no one ever eat fruit from you *to the end of this age*."* Such a translation leaves open the possibility of a future reversal, and Mark, in a later chapter, refers to the fig tree in bloom (13:28). The possibility of such a reversal also fits better with one of the first things Mark says about the tree: "It was not the time for figs" (11:13). As we have noted before, the Wisdom writings are especially attuned to the idea that human matters are not permanent but seasonable.

The conversation that Mark gives between Jesus and Peter regarding the tree (11:20-25) gives hope for a different season. Peter says, "The fig tree that you cursed has withered" (11:21). Jesus' response, "Have faith in God" (11:22), is usually taken to mean that Jesus is telling Peter he could have the same power as Jesus. If one has been following Mark's view of Jesus, one sees that he always shows Jesus' power directed toward healing. So here it seems right to understand Jesus' reply as encouragement to have faith in the fig tree's restoration.

Such an understanding is bolstered by two things. First, the term "withered" should remind Mark's readers of the episode where Jesus healed the man with a withered arm (3:1-5). Second, Mark shows Jesus going on here to recommend not only prayer but forgiveness (11:24-25). By providing the context of forgiveness, Mark suggests the possibility of a renewed tree. And as we have just noted above, Mark shows us a renewed fig tree later on.

 Some scholars interpret the **barren fig tree cursed by Jesus** as a metaphor for Israel, basing their interpretation on similar imagery used by the prophets (e.g., Jer 8:13; Hos 9:10; Joel 1:7) and on a comparison between this episode in Mark and the parable of the barren fig tree found in Luke 13:6-9. The fig itself was traditionally considered by church fathers such as St. John Chrysostom as a symbol of charity and unity.

11:27-32 "By what power . . . ?" (11:28)

The chapter concludes with Mark giving a direct question from the Temple authorities about the source of Jesus' power. Mark then shows Jesus replying with a question that is also something of a riddle: "Was John's baptism of heavenly or of human origin?" (11:30). By showing the authorities' confusion in trying to answer it, Mark indicates their mistake in trying to divide the "human" from the "heavenly." Implied is Mark's view that the figure and actions of Jesus show that they belong together.

Summary of chapter 11

In chapter 10, Mark has shown Jesus teaching his disciples that they should not seek worldly power but rather should follow him in seeking "not be served but to serve." In this chapter, Mark shows the kind of power Jesus does possess. He shows him to be at once forceful and humble.

In the opening verses, Mark shows Jesus entering Jerusalem to the acclaim of crowds, yet riding on a donkey. Through the language he uses to describe Jesus, Mark relates him both to Zechariah's peacemaking king and to Simon Maccabeus in his act of taking back the Temple. Through his description of Jesus' actions in the Temple, Mark further indicates Jesus' relationship to Simon's "cleansing" of the Temple. Through his quotations from Jesus' teaching, Mark places Jesus simultaneously in the tradition of prophetic reform of the Temple (like Jeremiah) and in the tradition of the prophetic vision of restoration of the Temple and universal prayer (like Isaiah).

By enclosing the symbolic action in the Temple with two episodes involving the fig tree, Mark further symbolizes the relationship between Jesus and power. In the first episode, Mark shows Jesus cursing the tree in much the same way that God cursed the ground in Genesis. It is another episode in which Mark shows Jesus reflecting God's action in the Hebrew Bible. Yet in the second episode, Mark shows Jesus encouraging Peter to "have faith" in its restoration. Mark's view is parallel to Isaiah's view of God reversing the original curse and restoring the earth.

Through this conversation with Peter, Mark indicates that Jesus is pointing to the power to move or transform things through faith and prayer and, above all, forgiveness. Through the further exchange between Jesus and the Temple authorities, Mark suggests how it is God's power, especially the power to forgive, that unites the human and the heavenly.

JESUS AS WISDOM IN THE TEMPLE

Mark 12:1-44

12:1-13 Parable of the vineyard

It is striking that Mark shows Jesus once again speaking in parables, a style he has not shown him using since chapter 4. This parable is clearly an allegory, but it is also shaped by pieces of interweaving Scripture. The vineyard as a metaphor for Israel occurs in Isaiah, Jere-

---

CHAPTER 12

Parable of the Tenants

¹He began to speak to them in parables. "A man planted a vineyard, put a hedge around it, dug a wine press, and built a tower. Then he leased it to tenant farmers and left on a journey. ²At the proper time he sent a servant to the tenants to obtain from them some of the produce of the vineyard. ³But they seized him, beat him, and sent him away empty-handed. ⁴Again he sent them another servant. And that one they beat over the head and treated shamefully. ⁵He sent yet another whom they killed. So, too, many others; some they beat, others they killed. ⁶He had one other

continue

---

miah, Ezekiel, Hosea, and the Song of Songs. In this long tradition, God creates a vineyard that he loves. He is sometimes angry at it, but in the end God always restores it. The opening verses here echo, in a condensed way, the "Vineyard Song" in Isaiah:

> My friend had a vineyard
>   on a fertile hillside;
> He spaded it, cleared it of stones,
>   and planted the choicest vines;
> Within it he built a watchtower,
>   and hewed out a wine press.
> Then he waited for the crop of grapes,
>   but it yielded rotten grapes (Isa 5:1-2).

In Isaiah's song, the "friend" is God, and "the vineyard of the Lord of hosts is the house of Israel" (Isa 5:7). God is angry at his vineyard for only yielding "rotten grapes," and he threatens to destroy it (Isa 5:5-6). Much later in Isaiah, when God proclaims a "new heavens and a new earth," he also promises a new vineyard (Isa 65:17-21).

It is important to realize that although Mark is clearly alluding to the first passage in Isaiah, he is not repeating it. There are key differences: the vineyard here is not yielding

Lesson Two

> to send, a beloved son. He sent him to them last of all, thinking, 'They will respect my son.' ⁷But those tenants said to one another, 'This is the heir. Come, let us kill him, and the inheritance will be ours.' ⁸So they seized him and killed him, and threw him out of the vineyard. ⁹What [then] will the owner of the vineyard do? He will come, put the tenants to death, and give the vineyard to others. ¹⁰Have you not read this scripture passage:
>
> > 'The stone that the builders rejected
> > has become the cornerstone;
> > ¹¹by the Lord has this been done,
> > and it is wonderful in our eyes'?"
>
> ¹²They were seeking to arrest him, but they feared the crowd, for they realized that he had addressed the parable to them. So they left him and went away.
>
> *continue*

"wild grapes" but a good harvest. The anger of the vineyard owner is therefore not directed at the vineyard, but at the tenants who are keeping him from gathering it (12:8b). What we have in Mark is thus not the same plot line as in Isaiah but a rather different story. We cannot hastily conclude (as many have) that it is about God's anger at Israel, because if we are reading carefully, we see that the vineyard (Israel) is not the cause of God's distress.

At the conclusion of the parable, Mark tells us that Jesus said that the owner of the vineyard would "put the tenants to death, and give the vineyard to others" (12:9). Mark then shows Jesus quoting Psalm 118:22:

> The stone that the builders rejected
> has become the cornerstone.

Christians of a later time came to identify "the cornerstone" with Christ, and so they interpreted this parable to mean that God would take his vineyard from Jews and give it to Christians. But in the tradition flourishing in Mark's time, the psalm was sung at Passover as a way of rejoicing that Israel, the enslaved people, had become the cornerstone of a nation covenanted to God. Knowing this fact, we need to carefully reexamine all the terms of the parable.

First of all, who are the tenants? The word "tenants" suggests those who have a commercial interest in the property, not a personal one. They are distinguished in the story from the landlord's "servants," whom they beat up and send away, and from his "beloved son," whom they kill. In biblical tradition, a prophet is usually described as God's servant. Israel itself is known as God's servant and also as God's beloved son. The "tenants" are hostile to the servants and the son, and obstructionist in regard to the vineyard. In short, they are hostile to Israel.

The parable, then, is not directed against Israel but against those who would destroy it. Israel, as God's vineyard, is fruitful, but hostile hirelings are preventing God's harvest. God promises to take back the vineyard from them and give it to others who will allow it to come to harvest.

Mark then says, "They were seeking to arrest him, but they feared the crowd, for they realized that he had addressed the parable to them" (12:12). Mark does not explicitly identify whom he means by "them," and there is no direct antecedent. In the following verse, Mark says that "They sent some Pharisees and Herodians to him . . . ." (12:13), so we know that he could not mean either of those two groups. The only plausible group left are the Temple authorities who were questioning Jesus in chapter 11—"the chief priests, the scribes, and the elders" (11:27). In terms of what we know of the historical situation of the Temple in the time of Jesus, the parable is a transparent allegory of the corruption of the Temple by Rome and its Jewish collaborators—that is, the chief priests and some of their associates who had sold out to Rome.

In addition, the reference to the landowner's "beloved son," of course, also suggests Jesus himself, who has been referred to by this phrase twice before at key moments in Mark's Gospel—at his baptism and his transfiguration

(1:11; 9:7). In the baptism scene, we have suggested, Jesus is God's "beloved son" in the sense of being a "second Adam," giving hope for a renewed humanity. In the transfiguration scene, Mark shows Jesus addressed by God as "my beloved son" in terms of his inner radiance, which images God's own. At the same time, it is a scene in which Mark shows Jesus in conversation with Elijah and Moses, that is, he shows him in conversation with the greatest prophets of Jewish tradition.

We have noted before that in a Markan triad, the middle episode is the most illuminating one. The transfiguration scene seems to imply that Jesus represents the teachings of Israel in the same way as Moses and Elijah did. So here in this vineyard parable, Jesus stands allied with religious Israel. In predicting the death of "the beloved son" at the hands of outsiders hostile to Israel, the parable is predicting simultaneously the death of Jesus and the destruction of the Temple. By means of this parable, Mark shows how both were destroyed by perverted power. The parable is a fitting conclusion to the discussion of power that runs through both chapters 10 and 11.

12:13-37 The four questions

In this section, Mark shows Jesus answering four questions about the Torah, the first five books of the Bible, or the teachings of Moses. In biblical thought, the Torah was equated with Wisdom. We have spoken earlier about how, in many different ways, Mark presents Jesus as God's Wisdom. So here, as he shows Jesus in the Temple answering questions about the Torah, Mark suggests that he is responding as Wisdom itself.

It is worth noting, moreover, that the questions involve different schools of thought within Early Judaism—Pharisees, Sadducees, and scribes. David Daube, a Jewish scholar, has suggested that they also represent the four questions asked by four sons in an ancient family liturgy for Passover. The first question is asked by a righteous son on a point of law. The second question is a mocking one, asked by a wicked son. The third question comes from a

> ### Paying Taxes to the Emperor
>
> [13]They sent some Pharisees and Herodians to him to ensnare him in his speech. [14]They came and said to him, "Teacher, we know that you are a truthful man and that you are not concerned with anyone's opinion. You do not regard a person's status but teach the way of God in accordance with the truth. Is it lawful to pay the census tax to Caesar or not? Should we pay or should we not pay?" [15]Knowing their hypocrisy he said to them, "Why are you testing me? Bring me a denarius to look at." [16]They brought one to him and he said to them, "Whose image and inscription is this?" They replied to him, "Caesar's." [17]So Jesus said to them, "Repay to Caesar what belongs to Caesar and to God what belongs to God." They were utterly amazed at him.
>
> *continue*

pious son. Finally, the father of the family gives instruction to a fourth son, who does not know how to ask.

12:13-17 The first response: "Whose image?"

Jesus' response to the Pharisees' question about the lawfulness of the Temple tax is often treated as a statement on the separation of church and state. One of the main causes of Jewish anger at the Caesars was their attempt (like Antiochus IV before them) to put their own image in the Temple. Jesus' response implies that Caesar's image has no place there.

More important, however, is how Mark uses this question (as he has earlier in his Gospel) to illumine Jesus' teaching on some key passage in the Bible. In this case, when Jesus responds to the Pharisees' question with his own question, "Whose image and inscription is this?" (12:16), there is more at stake than money. Mark shows Jesus using language that would have reminded his audience of the most important verse in Genesis: "God created [human beings] in his image" (1:27).

> ### The Question about the Resurrection
>
> ¹⁸Some Sadducees, who say there is no resurrection, came to him and put this question to him, ¹⁹saying, "Teacher, Moses wrote for us, 'If someone's brother dies, leaving a wife but no child, his brother must take the wife and raise up descendants for his brother.' ²⁰Now there were seven brothers. The first married a woman and died, leaving no descendants. ²¹So the second married her and died, leaving no descendants, and the third likewise. ²²And the seven left no descendants. Last of all the woman also died. ²³At the resurrection [when they arise] whose wife will she be? For all seven had been married to her." ²⁴Jesus said to them, "Are you not misled because you do not know the scriptures or the power of God? ²⁵When they rise from the dead, they neither marry nor are given in marriage, but they are like the angels in heaven. ²⁶As for the dead being raised, have you not read in the Book of Moses, in the passage about the bush, how God told him, 'I am the God of Abraham, [the] God of Isaac, and [the] God of Jacob'? ²⁷He is not God of the dead but of the living. You are greatly misled."
>
> *continue*

What the response implies is this: Caesar's image may be on the coin, but God's image is inscribed on every human being. Jesus' response is first of all a theological one. The theological answer, moreover, touches the core of Mark's Gospel, because Mark has shown Jesus himself to be the image of God.

12:18-27 The second response: "He is not God of the dead but of the living"

The Sadducees were a group particularly in league with the Temple priests. Unlike the Pharisees, they questioned belief in immortality, and their narrative here is designed to make that belief seem ridiculous. Mark shows Jesus responding in a way that emphasizes God as the Creator. First, he shows Jesus pointing to "the scriptures" and "the power of God" (12:24). Then he shows Jesus spelling out what he has in mind by quoting God's words to Moses at the burning bush: "I am the God of Abraham, [the] God of Isaac, and [the] God of Jacob" (12:26). The meaning of the reply is not obvious, and one has to read between the lines. But Jesus' response implies that by speaking of the patriarchs in the present tense, God indicates that they are still alive, because "He is not God of the dead but of the living" (12:27). Mark shows Jesus suggesting that belief in the Scriptures would lead one to belief in resurrection. Mark also quotes Jesus as saying twice to the Sadducees that they are "misled" (12:24, 27). He implies that not to believe in resurrection is to limit God's power.

To further unpack this passage, Jesus' response seems to be saying that if one believes that God had the power to create life, one should believe that God has the power to re-create it. This point of view is in keeping with the way Mark has depicted Jesus, throughout his Gospel, as healing and restoring life. It is in keeping with the transfiguration scene, in which Mark shows Elijah and Moses fully alive. It is in keeping with the way Mark continually points to Jesus' own resurrection.

12:28-34 The third response: "You shall love the Lord your God . . . ."

The third question is asked by "one of the scribes" (12:28), a group particularly versed in Scripture. The scribe asks the most basic question: "Which is the first of all the commandments?" (12:28).

In his reply, Mark shows Jesus weaving together three essential parts of Judaism. The first part, "Hear, O Israel! The Lord our God is Lord alone" (12:29), is the central "creed" of Judaism, that is, it is an assertion of Jews' central belief in one God. It has always been at the heart of Jewish worship. The second part, "You shall love the Lord your God with all your heart, with all your soul, with all your mind, and with all your strength" (12:30), is a direct quotation from Deuteronomy (6:5). The third part, "You shall love your neighbor as yourself" (12:31), is a direct quotation from Leviticus (19:18).

By interweaving these three parts, Mark shows Jesus speaking as a scribe himself, that is, as a teacher of Scripture. Mark shows Jesus using a method typical of Jewish Scripture scholars and Wisdom teachers of the first century. The effect of this interweaving is to suggest that love of God implies love of neighbor and that both together are what constitute true worship.

It is striking that Mark shows Jesus and the scribe to be in perfect agreement. He shows the scribe repeating what Jesus has said, only adding another quotation from Scripture to further support it: " 'To love your neighbor as yourself' is worth more than all burnt offerings and sacrifices" (12:33).

The last part of the scribe's comment is an allusion to Psalm 40:7-9:

> Sacrifice and offering you do not want. . . .
> Holocaust and sin-offering you do not request;
>   so I said, "See; I come . . .
> I delight to do your will, my God."

Mark shows that the scribe uses the same method as Jesus, bringing together different parts of the Hebrew Bible to illuminate their meaning.

Mark further indicates the harmony between Jesus and the scribe when he quotes Jesus saying to him approvingly, "You are not far from the kingdom of God" (12:34). The incident stands out because through it Mark shows that Jesus was not at odds with *all* the scribes and Temple authorities. On the contrary, Mark shows Jesus to be in perfect agreement with one who taught the central tenets of Judaism.

The **scribes** in Jesus' time were members of the intellectual elite within Jewish society. Their reputation for scholarship was based on an intimate knowledge of the Mosaic law, which formed the chief subject of their study. Scribes were also considered authorities on the oral traditions of Judaism, which evolved from various interpretations and explanations of the written law and governed much of Jewish life and worship. The scribes' unsurpassed knowledge of the Torah assured them an important leadership role among the Jewish people.

The Greatest Commandment

²⁸One of the scribes, when he came forward and heard them disputing and saw how well he had answered them, asked him, "Which is the first of all the commandments?" ²⁹Jesus replied, "The first is this: 'Hear, O Israel! The Lord our God is Lord alone! ³⁰You shall love the Lord your God with all your heart, with all your soul, with all your mind, and with all your strength.' ³¹The second is this: 'You shall love your neighbor as yourself.' There is no other commandment greater than these." ³²The scribe said to him, "Well said, teacher. You are right in saying, 'He is One and there is no other than he.' ³³And 'to love him with all your heart, with all your understanding, with all your strength, and to love your neighbor as yourself' is worth more than all burnt offerings and sacrifices." ³⁴And when Jesus saw that [he] answered with understanding, he said to him, "You are not far from the kingdom of God." And no one dared to ask him any more questions.

The Question about David's Son

³⁵As Jesus was teaching in the temple area he said, "How do the scribes claim that the Messiah is the son of David? ³⁶David himself, inspired by the holy Spirit, said:
'The Lord said to my lord,
"Sit at my right hand
 until I place your enemies under your feet."'

³⁷David himself calls him 'lord'; so how is he his son?" [The] great crowd heard this with delight.

continue

12:35-37 The fourth response: "How is he [the messiah] his [David's] son?"

In this passage, Mark shows Jesus posing a riddle about the meaning of "the messiah." He does so by continuing to juxtapose one Scripture passage with another. In this instance, he juxtaposes the tradition based on God's promise to David in the second book of Samuel with a popular interpretation of Psalm

Lesson Two

> **Denunciation of the Scribes**
>
> ³⁸In the course of his teaching he said, "Beware of the scribes, who like to go around in long robes and accept greetings in the marketplaces, ³⁹seats of honor in synagogues, and places of honor at banquets. ⁴⁰They devour the houses of widows and, as a pretext, recite lengthy prayers. They will receive a very severe condemnation."
>
> *continue*

110. In the passage from 2 Samuel, God says to David:

> I will raise up your offspring after you, sprung from your loins, and I will establish his kingdom. He it is who shall build a house for my name, and I will establish his royal throne forever. I will be a father to him, and he shall be a son to me. . . . Your house and your kingdom are firm forever before me; your throne shall be firmly established forever (2 Sam 7:12b-14, 16).

In the first century, all the psalms were popularly attributed to David, so he was considered the speaker in Psalm 110. In its opening verse, the words "my lord" were interpreted as a reference to a coming messiah who would be victorious for Israel. Mark shows Jesus putting these two things together and suggesting that they don't add up—that is, he is asking: If the coming messiah is a son of David, how come David calls him "my lord"?

There is no answer to this riddle. By having Jesus pose this riddle, Mark is not intent on giving answers but on raising questions. The riddle raises a question about popular understandings of "the messiah." Earlier in his Gospel, Mark shows that Peter has an understanding that Jesus does not share. Peter thinks that if Jesus is "the messiah," he cannot suffer and die. And as we have seen, Jesus reproaches him (8:29-33). Here Mark shows Jesus using Scripture to reveal the fault line in the tradition. By this means, Mark shows how

Jesus raised questions in the minds of his audience. Mark shakes up the popular definition of "the messiah" so that he can dramatize that Jesus is a "messiah" in an unconventional sense.

12:38-44 The rich and the poor in the Temple

Mark concludes the chapter with a contrast between those who use the Temple for their own profit and those who give to it their last coin. The episode sums up and illumines the theme of wealth versus poverty that has run throughout the last three chapters.

We have just noted that Mark shows Jesus in perfect agreement with one of the scribes. But here he shows Jesus denouncing those scribes who use their religion for self-aggrandizement. It is important to see that the scribes who seek "seats of honor" are not unlike James and John, who asked to sit at Jesus' right and left in his glory (10:37). By means of the echo, Mark reminds us of Jesus' teaching that "whoever wishes to be first among you will be the slave of all" (10:44). In addition to seeking glory, we learn, these Temple authorities make venal profit off the needs of poor widows (12:40). The language that Mark shows Jesus using to describe their action—"they *devour* the houses of widows" (emphasis added)—suggests that their greed is the reverse of the nurturing habits of Jesus himself.

The episode of the poor widow has several functions. First of all, it clarifies Jesus' anger at the money changers (11:15-17). By showing Jesus' approval of the widow's contribution to the Temple treasury, Mark indicates that it was not money in the Temple per se that caused Jesus' anger. Rather, as the condemnation of the greedy scribes shows, Jesus was angered by those who used the Temple money for themselves.

At the same time, when Mark shows Jesus praising the poor widow because "she, from her poverty, has contributed all she had" (12:44), he also shows him echoing his instruction to the rich man to sell all he has (10:21). The widow's total self-giving embodies the commandment to "love the Lord your God with all your heart, with all your soul, with all your mind, and with all your strength" (12:30).

Summary of chapter 12

The chapter is unified around the theme of wholehearted love of God versus religion perverted by greed and hypocrisy. The parable of the vineyard contrasts the venal tenants of the vineyard with the vineyard owner's servants and "beloved son." It is a transparent allegory, contrasting the present authorities in the Temple—the Romans and their hirelings—with the prophets and with Jesus.

The parable makes use of the vineyard tradition in the Hebrew Bible, especially Isaiah, to indicate the similarities and differences between Israel's situation now and in the past. As in the past, God is not able to reap from his vineyard (Israel) the harvest he wants from it. Unlike the past, the cause of this is not the vineyard itself but the obstructions placed in the way by the greedy and hostile occupier of the vineyard (Rome).

These "tenants" want whatever "inheritance" there is for themselves. The narrative of the killing of the beloved son, together with the image of the ungathered harvest, suggests that those who now occupy the vineyard are responsible both for the killing of Jesus and for the destruction of the Temple. The quotation from Psalm 110 in the conclusion of the parable suggests that God will vindicate his people (Israel) as he has before.

When Jesus tells this parable, Mark depicts him again as a Wisdom teacher. In the rest of the chapter, Mark shows Jesus engaged in interpreting the meaning of Scripture to various groups of Jewish scholars in the Temple. By doing this, Mark suggests (as he has earlier) that Jesus is Wisdom itself.

As Wisdom in the Temple, Jesus responds to four types of questions about Jewish teaching. The first question puts forward the relationship between the Temple and worldly power. Jesus' response suggests that worldly power does not belong in the Temple. It also suggests that human beings, as bearers of God's image, belong wholly to God. The second question puts forward the relationship between God and death. Jesus' response indicates that God is concerned with life, not death. God the Creator has the power to go on creating. The third question puts forward the relationship between love of God and love of neighbor. Jesus and the scribe agree that they are inextricably woven together. Love of neighbor (as the Psalms and Prophets have said) is the truest way of loving God. The last question takes the form of a riddle that Jesus himself asks about the meaning of God's "messiah." The riddle raises questions about the conventional understandings of the term and so prepares for an unconventional one.

All of Jesus' responses bear on his identity in Mark's Gospel. Mark presents Jesus as image of God, as one who lives beyond death, as one who has come "not to be served but to serve" (10:45), and as unconventional messiah.

These responses also indicate the kind of Temple reform Jesus stands for. In conclusion, Mark sums up that reform by the contrast Jesus makes between the venal and hypocritical Temple authorities, who use the Temple for their own purposes, and the poor widow, who gives all that she has to sustain it.

The Poor Widow's Contribution

[41]He sat down opposite the treasury and observed how the crowd put money into the treasury. Many rich people put in large sums. [42]A poor widow also came and put in two small coins worth a few cents. [43]Calling his disciples to himself, he said to them, "Amen, I say to you, this poor widow put in more than all the other contributors to the treasury. [44]For they have all contributed from their surplus wealth, but she, from her poverty, has contributed all she had, her whole livelihood."

Lesson Two

EXPLORING LESSON TWO

1. How do the Old Testament passages of Zechariah 9:9-10 and 1 Maccabees 13:47-52 shed light on Mark's depiction of Jesus' triumphal entry into Jerusalem (11:1-11)? (See Matt 21:5.)

2. How would you explain Jesus' reasons for cursing the fig tree (11:11-14, 20-21)?

3. How do the passages Jesus quotes from Isaiah (56:7) and Jeremiah (7:11) help explain why Jesus was disrupting normal activity in the Temple area (11:15-19)?

4. When have you experienced the power of prayer (11:22-26)? What do you think makes prayer most effective or powerful?

5. Why wouldn't Jesus tell the chief priests and scribes where he obtained the authority for his actions (11:27-33)? What message might he have communicated by refusing to answer?

Lesson Two

6. What would so upset the priests and scribes that they would want to arrest Jesus for telling the parable of the vineyard and the tenants (12:1-12)? (See Isa 5:11-7; Jer 12:10-11.)

7. Where do you see tensions in modern society over giving to Caesar what is due to Caesar and giving to God what is due to God (12:13-17)?

8. In Mark 12:35-37, Jesus quotes Psalm 110:1 to question the popular interpretation of the messiah as the son of David. How is this same passage from Psalm 110 used elsewhere in the New Testament? (See Acts 2:32-36; Heb 1:5-14.)

9. What acts of generosity have you witnessed that have encouraged you to also be generous (12:38-44)?

CLOSING PRAYER

Prayer

"He is not God of the dead but of the living."
(Mark 12:27)

Heavenly Father, through the passion and death of your son Jesus, you have given us the gift of eternal life. We pray today for the souls of all those who have died in Christ, those we dearly love, and those who may have died unloved and are not remembered. May all the faithful departed rest in your peace, especially . . .

LESSON THREE

Mark 13–14

Begin your personal study and group discussion with a simple and sincere prayer such as:

Prayer

Lord Jesus, as we read this Gospel, may we hear your words and meditate on your life with open hearts and alert minds. May our time of study and sharing strengthen our faith in you, the source of all truth and wisdom.

Read the Bible text of Mark 13–14 found in the outside columns of pages 46–63, highlighting what stands out to you.

Read the accompanying commentary to add to your understanding.

Respond to the questions on pages 64–65, Exploring Lesson Three.

The Closing Prayer on page 66 is for your personal use and may be used at the end of group discussion.

Lesson Three

> **CHAPTER 13**
>
> *The Destruction of the Temple Foretold*
>
> ¹As he was making his way out of the temple area one of his disciples said to him, "Look, teacher, what stones and what buildings!" ²Jesus said to him, "Do you see these great buildings? There will not be one stone left upon another that will not be thrown down."
>
> *continue*

JESUS AS PROPHET IN THE TEMPLE

Mark 13:1-37

13:1-2 The prophecy of the destruction of the Temple

In chapters 11 and 12, Mark has shown Jesus pointing to the spiritual devastation of the Temple. Here he speaks of its coming physical destruction. Both kinds of speech belong to the role of the prophet. We have a tendency today to restrict the word "prophet" to one who makes predictions about the future. But the biblical prophets were not soothsayers. They were messengers of God, reminding the people of God's past word in Scripture and, in the light of it, conveying God's present word on human behavior. They were, in fact, preachers.

The prevailing theme of the prophets is the need for Temple reform. By this they did not so much mean reform of liturgical practices but of people's way of living. They were constantly calling the people back to their commitment to the covenant. They identified the breaking of any of the commandments with idolatry. For example, Jeremiah's "Temple sermon" (see p. 32) equates adultery and perjury with the worship of Baal. They always preached, moreover, in times when Israel was in crisis—either under attack by foreign powers or actually occupied by them. Every foreign power that conquered Jerusalem also took over the Temple. So in such times (which constituted most of Israel's biblical history), the danger of idolatry from within was compounded by foreign influences from without. As a consequence, the prophets warned the people again and again about succumbing to false gods as well as about neglecting their obligations to love their neighbors as themselves.

The Temple building functioned as a key image in these warnings. The prophets expressed God's displeasure with the people by saying either that God would destroy the Temple or that God would leave the Temple. Many scholars think that these imaginative warnings were not so much predicting disaster to the Temple as reflecting on it after the fact. Take Jeremiah, for example. The Temple was destroyed by Babylon in 586 B.C.E., the time of Jeremiah, and the people lived in exile from Jerusalem until 539. When Jeremiah, therefore, tells the people that it is God's will for them to submit to Babylon, is he looking ahead, or is he trying to reassure the exiles that God had a plan in allowing their disaster? Many scholars think it was the latter.

All this background is relevant to the prophecy that Mark shows Jesus making here. For the second time in Jewish history, the Temple was destroyed—this time by the Romans in the year 70 C.E., forty years after the death of Jesus but in the lifetime of Mark. It had a traumatic effect on everyone associated with the Jewish community, including those

Jews who were followers of Jesus. Most scholars date the Gospel of Mark around that time, either just before or just after. Mark portrays Jesus, as we have seen, in the role of a prophet, preaching about the corruption of Temple worship. The prophetic tradition raises this question: When Mark shows Jesus saying that the Temple would be destroyed, is he suggesting that Jesus in fact predicted its destruction, or is he imaginatively projecting how Jesus as prophet reflected on its meaning?

In any case, the chapter is carefully designed. Mark opens the chapter by citing the disciples' admiration for the Temple. Their wonder at the great buildings expresses a long tradition of reverence for the Temple as the dwelling place of God. Mark cites Jesus' reply without indicating his tone of voice. Many have assumed that Mark shows Jesus to be angry at the Temple, but we have seen that his anger is tempered by the prophetic vision of reform.

13:4 and 13:32 "When will this happen?"

At the time that Mark was composing, there was a large body of Jewish writings known as "apocalyptic." They were characterized by a number of things. They warned of a final disaster that in some way took the form of a battle between good and evil, that is, directly between God and Satan, or between good and evil nations, or between good and evil forces. (For example, the Dead Sea Scrolls speak of a final clash between "the sons of darkness" and the "sons of light.") They made precise predictions about the time that the world would end. They also projected that there would be particular signs that the end was about to happen. The question raised by the disciples here—"Tell us, when will this happen, and what sign will there be when all these things are about to come to an end?" (13:4)—is typical of these writings. Mark does not give Jesus' reply for many verses, and when he does, he shows him giving an answer that does not fit the apocalyptic perspective: "But of that day or hour, no one knows, neither the angels in heaven, nor the Son, but only the Father" (13:32). This exchange functions as the frame for the chapter.

The Signs of the End

³As he was sitting on the Mount of Olives opposite the temple area, Peter, James, John, and Andrew asked him privately, ⁴"Tell us, when will this happen, and what sign will there be when all these things are about to come to an end?" ⁵Jesus began to say to them, "See that no one deceives you. ⁶Many will come in my name saying, 'I am he,' and they will deceive many. ⁷When you hear of wars and reports of wars do not be alarmed; such things must happen, but it will not yet be the end. ⁸Nation will rise against nation and kingdom against kingdom. There will be earthquakes from place to place and there will be famines. These are the beginnings of the labor pains.

The Coming Persecution

⁹"Watch out for yourselves. They will hand you over to the courts. You will be beaten in synagogues. You will be arraigned before governors and kings because of me, as a witness before them. ¹⁰But the gospel must first be preached to all nations. ¹¹When they lead you away and hand you over, do not worry beforehand about what you are to say. But say whatever will be given to you

continue

13:5-13 Instructions to the disciples

Mark shows that instead of replying right away to the disciples' question, Jesus instructs them on how to behave in the face of coming disaster. These instructions are a mixture of many things, and they need to be looked at carefully.

Some of what Mark shows Jesus saying are generalized clichés taken from contemporary writing about the end of time. These include the warnings about "wars and reports of wars" (13:7), about nation rising against nation (13:8a), about "earthquakes" (13:8b), about how "brother will hand over brother to death" (13:12).

But most of the warnings Mark places in Jesus' mouth are ones that would only have

Lesson Three

> at that hour. For it will not be you who are speaking but the holy Spirit. ¹²Brother will hand over brother to death, and the father his child; children will rise up against parents and have them put to death. ¹³You will be hated by all because of my name. But the one who perseveres to the end will be saved.
>
> **The Great Tribulation**
>
> ¹⁴"When you see the desolating abomination standing where he should not (let the reader understand), then those in Judea must flee to the mountains, ¹⁵[and] a person on a housetop must not go down or enter to get anything out of his house, ¹⁶and a person in a field must not return to get his cloak. ¹⁷Woe to pregnant women and nursing mothers in those days. ¹⁸Pray that this does not happen in winter. ¹⁹For those times will have tribulation such as has not been since the beginning of God's creation until now, nor ever
>
> *continue*

had meaning for Mark's own community in the year 70 or later. For example, Jesus' warning that "Many will come in my name saying, 'I am he'" (13:6) makes most sense after Jesus' death. Indeed, earlier Mark has shown Jesus refusing to stop someone healing in his name, saying, "Whoever is not against us is for us" (9:40). Similarly, Jesus' warning that "They will hand you over to the courts. You will be beaten in synagogues. You will be arraigned before governors and kings because of me" (13:9) does not apply to the disciples of Jesus' time but to his later followers.

It becomes clear that Mark is speaking to his own time when he shows Jesus saying, "But the gospel must first be preached to all the nations" (13:10). So, too, the advice that immediately follows this statement makes sense if it is seen as directed to Mark's community: "When they lead you away and hand you over, do not worry beforehand about what you are to say. But say whatever will be given to you at that hour. For it will not be you who are speaking but the holy Spirit" (13:11). Finally, the warning "You will be hated by all because of my name" (13:13a) suggests what was happening in Mark's time, not in that of Jesus.

It is important to realize that Mark is addressing two different periods of time. Otherwise, we might think that the hatred and persecution of Jesus' followers happened while Jesus was still alive. But we know historically that this was not the case. And in other parts of his Gospel, Mark has shown that while some of those in power were hostile to Jesus, the crowds followed him. It is Mark's community, living after the double trauma of the death of Jesus and the destruction of the Temple, that needs encouragement to persevere to the end (13:13b).

13:14-27 An apocalyptic end?

This description of the end again makes use of phrases used in apocalyptic writings of the time. These include the warning to flee to the mountains (13:14), and not to go back to one's house (13:16), the lament for those who are pregnant "in those days" (13:17), and the admonition to "Pray that this does not happen in winter" (13:18).

The reference to "tribulation such as has not been" (13:19) is taken verbatim from Daniel 12:1, where it is indeed predicting a final disaster that will bring about an eternal separation of the good from the wicked:

> Some shall live forever,
> others shall be an everlasting horror and disgrace (Dan 12:2; NAB).

As in other apocalyptic literature, this moment of doom is precisely timed. In this case, the doom is related to "the desolating abomination": "From the time that the daily sacrifice is abolished and the desolating abomination is set up, there shall be one thousand two hundred and ninety days" (Dan 12:11).

The "desolating abomination" is Daniel's veiled way of speaking about Antiochus's sacrilegious act of placing an image of himself in the Temple. Mark clearly shows Jesus referring to the same act when he uses the very same phrase (13:14a) and then emphasizes that the reference is to a written work ("let the reader understand," 13:14b). By showing that Jesus quotes the book of Daniel, Mark suggests that Jesus, too, perceives sacrilege in the Temple as the cause of the tribulations to come. Only in Mark's time, the veiled reference to sacrilege would have been to that of the Romans.

But Mark also shows that Jesus' perspective is different from that of Daniel and the other apocalyptic writings. He does this in many different ways. First, while Jesus warns, in typical apocalyptic language, of "wars" and "earthquakes" and "famines" (13:7-8), he also comments, "These are the beginnings of the labor pains" (13:8b). The image of "labor pains" or "birth pangs" was often associated with a time when God's kingdom would prevail.

Second, Mark shows Jesus reassuring his followers that God will shorten the days of tribulation (13:20). The description that follows of a darkened sun and stars "falling from the sky" (13:25) also has apocalyptic parallels, but the edge is softened here by the suggestion that this shaking of the heavens is part of God's act of mercy.

Third, Mark shows Jesus telling his disciples that he, the second Adam ("son of Adam" or "son of man"), will return in glory to gather his elect "from the end of the earth to the end of the sky" (13:26-27). Mark has shown Jesus speaking before about his own rising from the dead, but it is the first time that he has shown him promising his disciples some future glory.

In all these ways, Mark shows that while Jesus uses some apocalyptic terms, he does not share that perspective. In chapter 4, we looked at the way Mark shows Jesus telling an apocalyptic parable (the sower), and then two more parables that reverse its meaning (the seed growing secretly and the mustard seed). In the

> will be. ²⁰If the Lord had not shortened those days, no one would be saved; but for the sake of the elect whom he chose, he did shorten the days. ²¹If anyone says to you then, 'Look, here is the Messiah! Look, there he is!' do not believe it. ²²False messiahs and false prophets will arise and will perform signs and wonders in order to mislead, if that were possible, the elect. ²³Be watchful! I have told it all to you beforehand.
>
> ### The Coming of the Son of Man
>
> ²⁴"But in those days after that tribulation
>
> the sun will be darkened,
> and the moon will not give its light,
> ²⁵and the stars will be falling from the sky,
> and the powers in the heavens will be shaken.
>
> ²⁶And then they will see 'the Son of Man coming in the clouds' with great power and glory, ²⁷and then he will send out the angels and gather [his] elect from the four winds, from the end of the earth to the end of the sky.
>
> *continue*

same way here, Mark shows Jesus using the apocalyptic language of some contemporary writers in order to show how he differs from their point of view.

In Mark's Gospel, Jesus does not predict a final battle between good and evil, and he does not believe that anyone can calculate when the end will come. Instead, he says that the suffering to come should be understood as "labor pains" (13:8). He says that God will shorten the suffering (13:20). He says that beyond the suffering there will be glory (13:26). And he says that no one but God the Father can know the time of the end (13:32). Jesus also expresses a non-apocalyptic point of view in his reference to the fig tree and in his parable of the returning lord of the house.

Lesson Three

> ### The Lesson of the Fig Tree
>
> ²⁸"Learn a lesson from the fig tree. When its branch becomes tender and sprouts leaves, you know that summer is near. ²⁹In the same way, when you see these things happening, know that he is near, at the gates. ³⁰Amen, I say to you, this generation will not pass away until all these things have taken place. ³¹Heaven and earth will pass away, but my words will not pass away.
>
> ### Need for Watchfulness
>
> ³²"But of that day or hour, no one knows, neither the angels in heaven, nor the Son, but only the Father. ³³Be watchful! Be alert! You do not know when the time will come. ³⁴It is like a man traveling abroad. He leaves home and places his servants in charge, each with his work, and orders the gatekeeper to be on the watch. ³⁵Watch, therefore; you do not know when the lord of the house is coming, whether in the evening, or at midnight, or at cockcrow, or in the morning. ³⁶May he not come suddenly and find you sleeping. ³⁷What I say to you, I say to all: 'Watch!'"
>
> *continue*

13:28-31 The fig tree blooms again

In chapter 11, Mark shows Jesus first cursing a fig tree that was not in season (11:12-14), and later exhorting Peter to "have faith" in God's power to restore it (11:20-23). These episodes, we suggested, are best understood in terms of God's actions in the Hebrew Bible. In Genesis 3, God curses the ground, but in Isaiah, God reverses that curse (Isa 55:12-13; 65:17-25). Following a similar pattern, Mark shows Jesus speaking here of the fig tree once more in bloom. This image is particularly significant in the light of contemporary Jewish thought, where the fig tree coming back into bloom was considered a sign of God's kingdom.

13:32-37 The lord of the house returns

Mark shows Jesus telling a parable that has significance both for the time of Jesus and for the end time. It has immediate significance for Jesus' disciples because it warns of the lord of the house returning to his servants at "cockcrow" (13:35), a clear foreshadowing of the cockcrow that wakens Peter to remorse for having denied any knowledge of Jesus (14:30, 72).

This parable also bears a significant relationship to the parable of the vineyard (12:1-9). In that parable, the owner of the vineyard goes away and allows hired hands to tend his vineyard. In this parable, the owner also goes off, but he leaves his house in the charge of trusted servants. In both parables, the owner stands for God, and the vineyard or house represents the sacred space where God dwells. In the first parable, the sacred space is violated by hirelings; in the second parable, "the lord of the house" is on his way back home. The parable ends, as it were, with a question: What will the lord of the house find when he returns? And it explicitly ends with the advice to "watch" (13:33, 35, 37), an exhortation that belongs to the Wisdom traditions.

The exhortation to watchfulness appears three times in this chapter. It appears first when Jesus tells the disciples to "Watch out for yourselves" in regard to those who might deceive them (13:9). It occurs a second time in the context of Jesus' warning about "false messiahs and false prophets" (13:22-23). And it is repeated three times in connection with this parable—once at the beginning and twice at the end (13:33, 35, 37).

The word "watch" is the key word of the chapter. It belongs to the Wisdom traditions, because it is in those traditions that the acknowledgment of uncertainty is prized. It is wise to know what one does not know. So here Mark shows Jesus acknowledging that only God the Father can know when the end will come. Not knowing, one must be always on the watch.

> Jews and Romans reckoned **time** in different categories. While the Jewish day began at sundown (see Gen 1:5), the Roman day began at sunrise. The Romans divided the day and night into

two periods of twelve hours each, subdivided into three-hour segments. The Jewish day generally had three periods (see Ps 55:18), while the Roman day had four (first, third, sixth, and ninth hours). The Jewish night was divided into three "watches" while the Roman night was divided into four, which are mentioned in Mark 13:35: evening, midnight, cockcrow, and early morning.

Summary of chapter 13

The chapter is unified by the question about "signs." It is framed by the disciples' question that seeks definite signs as to when the end will come and by Jesus' reply that "No one knows," so they must always "watch." An apocalyptic question receives a non-apocalyptic reply.

In between, Mark shows Jesus countering what were conventionally considered the signs of God's coming judgment (war, earthquake, famine, family betrayal, death, and cosmic turmoil) with images that bring hope: giving birth, a merciful shortening of suffering, a glorious ingathering of the elect, a new season in which the fig tree blooms again. In this way, Mark shows Jesus countering the conventional fears of a coming apocalypse with suggestions of a new beginning.

The specific reference to "the beginning of God's creation" (13:19), even though it is made in the context of predicted suffering, is a reminder of God's purpose in creation to "look at everything [that God] had made" and find it "very good" (Gen 1:31). The very word "beginning" reminds Mark's readers of his persistent images of a new creation. The parable of the fig tree in bloom is one more of these images. It is a sign of return to the original Garden.

The glorious ingathering of Jesus as the "son of man" reinforces this sign. We have suggested before that the phrase "son of man" is best understood as "son of Adam." Jesus as "son of Adam" is also a second Adam. Mark presents him as a representative of humanity who has not fallen. As such, he is a representative who perfectly reflects human beings as

---

CHAPTER 14

The Conspiracy against Jesus

¹The Passover and the Feast of Unleavened Bread were to take place in two days' time. So the chief priests and the scribes were seeking a way to arrest him by treachery and put him to death. ²They said, "Not during the festival, for fear that there may be a riot among the people."

continue

God intended them to be at the beginning—as image of God.

The central "sign" of the chapter, of course, is the Temple itself. In chapters 11 and 12, Mark has shown Jesus using the language of the prophets to point to its corruption and to hope for its restoration. In this chapter, he shows Jesus borrowing the veiled words of the book of Daniel ("the desolating abomination") to point to the sacrilegious use of the Temple by the Romans. In the parable of "the lord of the house" returning home, he gives hope that God will come back to his dwelling place.

That hope, without certainty, brings the chapter to its concluding key word, the key word of Wisdom—"Watch!"

THE PASSION NARRATIVE, PART I: PREPARATIONS FOR DEATH AND LIFE

Mark 14:1-52

14:1-2 Preparation for betrayal

In these opening verses, Mark introduces the theme of betrayal that he interweaves throughout the chapter. The Feast of Passover, designed to celebrate the freedom of the people of God, is the setting for the plot to kill Jesus. By means of the plotters' remark that they had better not kill Jesus at the feast (14:2), Mark suggests the tension both between the feast and the plot and between the Temple authorities and the people.

The Anointing at Bethany

³When he was in Bethany reclining at table in the house of Simon the leper, a woman came with an alabaster jar of perfumed oil, costly genuine spikenard. She broke the alabaster jar and poured it on his head. ⁴There were some who were indignant. "Why has there been this waste of perfumed oil? ⁵It could have been sold for more than three hundred days' wages and the money given to the poor." They were infuriated with her. ⁶Jesus said, "Let her alone. Why do you make trouble for her? She has done a good thing for me. ⁷The poor you will always have with you, and whenever you wish you can do good to them, but you will not always have me. ⁸She has done what she could. She has

continue

14:3-9 Anointing: preparation for death and life

The next few verses present a counter theme. The setting is "the house of Simon the leper" (14:3). Mark introduces this figure without explanation. The reader only knows the name "Simon" in association with Peter (1:16, 29-30; 3:16). The only leper to appear before is the one cured in 1:40-45. Does Mark intend the reader to make some connection between this Simon and Simon Peter or between this leper and the one who was healed?

The mystery of the scene is compounded by the entry of an anonymous woman carrying an alabaster jar (14:3). Again, Mark makes no attempt to identify this woman. The reader, however, may have a subliminal memory of having encountered before this particular pairing of anonymous woman and leper. In Mark's account of Jesus' first miracles, he tells of Jesus healing "Simon's mother-in-law" (1:29-31), and then a leper (1:40-45). The name "Simon," transposed here to the leper, adds to the impression of déjà vu.

We noted earlier that Mark's language suggests that Jesus did not merely heal the woman physically but "raised her up"* (1:31) to a new status of ministry. It is one in which she "served"* others (1:31). And serving others is how Jesus describes his own way of life (10:45). The leper, too, receives more than a physical cure. Mark tells us that Jesus sent him back to the priest and so to his community. Once there, Mark says, he spread the word of Jesus to such an extent that Jesus could not "enter a town openly" (1:45).

Could it be, then, that Mark intends his readers to regard the woman and leper here as these two persons in their changed state? That supposition is supported by the fact that they act here in unconventional and extraordinary ways. Unlike most lepers, "Simon the leper" is able to open his home to a social gathering. Even more remarkable, Mark shows Jesus saying that what the anonymous woman has done will always be part of the gospel proclamation (14:9).

The leper disappears from the narrative while the woman preoccupies it. It is important to look carefully at how Mark describes her actions. A jar made of "alabaster" suggests something rare and valuable. The perfumed oil that it contains is described by two words, one of which is hard to translate. The first word means "pure"* (translated above as "genuine"). The other word does not appear in any other piece of writing; it is closest to the Greek word for "faith."* Mark is presenting his readers with a highly symbolic narrative in which the woman is bearing the costly oil of faith.

The woman proceeds to break the jar and pour out the oil (14:3b). The word Mark chooses for "break" here is no ordinary word, but one that means to "shatter" or "to destroy completely." By using it, Mark calls attention to the action. He suggests that this is not a casual or conventional sort of breaking. The word for "poured" has the sense of "poured out." In its root form, it is related to the word associated with a cultic pouring out of blood. Mark uses a variant of it later in the chapter when he describes Jesus saying, "This is my blood of the covenant, which is poured out for many" (14:24; or "will be shed for many" in NABRE). In fact, with hindsight one can see that the woman's gestures here of "breaking" and "pouring out" anticipate the gestures Mark shows Jesus making at the Last Supper. Mark makes the woman's extravagant gestures of breaking and pouring a symbolic foreshadowing of Jesus' extravagant gestures of giving his body to be broken and his blood to be poured out.

By showing the narrow-minded response of some present who view this extravagance as a "waste" (14:4-5), Mark sets the stage for Jesus' praise of this woman's act (14:8-9). Given the symbolic nature of the narrative, every word here is important. When Mark shows Jesus rebuking the protestors by saying, "Let her alone" (14:6), we hear an echo of the scene where Jesus rebukes those who were keeping back the children (10:13-14). When Mark shows Jesus saying, "She has done what she could" (14:8a), we hear an echo of Jesus' praise of the poor widow: "[She] contributed all she had" (12:44).

When Mark shows Jesus saying, "She has anticipated anointing my body for burial" (14:8b), we are forced to consider the different meanings of "anointing." Jesus speaks of anointing here in the context of consecrating the body for death. At the same time, Mark's readers would have been aware that Jesus was referred to as "messiah," a Hebrew word that means "the anointed one." In the Bible and other writings of the time, that term generally referred to someone who was sent to do God's work, and so it was a title associated with glory. But we have already seen that Mark shows Jesus rebuking Peter for making that association (8:29-33). Mark shows Jesus consistently teaching that God's anointed one should be associated instead with suffering and even death. In this episode in chapter 14, Mark dramatizes that meaning. Jesus becomes "the anointed one" in the context of death.

When Mark shows Jesus saying, "Wherever the gospel is proclaimed to the whole world, what she has done will be told in remembrance* of her" (14:9), what does Mark have in mind? We have suggested that Mark intends a connection between the woman's extravagant gestures of breaking and pouring and Jesus' gestures (later in this chapter) that symbolize his death. In other words, Mark makes her gestures anticipate the eucharistic gestures of Jesus. And

anticipated anointing my body for burial. ⁹Amen, I say to you, wherever the gospel is proclaimed to the whole world, what she has done will be told in memory of her."

The Betrayal by Judas

¹⁰Then Judas Iscariot, one of the Twelve, went off to the chief priests to hand him over to them.

continue

those gestures of breaking and pouring are the very ones that, according to Paul, Jesus asked his followers to do *"in remembrance"* of him (1 Cor 11:24-25, emphasis added).

The phrase expresses a concept important to Passover celebrations and also to celebrations of the Eucharist. In both instances, it conveys the sense of doing more than recalling a past event. Rather, it suggests a reliving of a past event in such a way that God's grace is not just recalled but made present. At the end of every Passover meal, the leader prays that God may grant the grace of freedom to every Jew here and now. In the same way, the presider at the Eucharist prays that the freeing grace of Jesus may be made present here and now. The eucharistic act of "remembrance" is not an act of recalling what Jesus did but of making it present once again.

When Mark gives his own account of the first Eucharist (14:22-26), his wording is close to that of Paul's account in First Corinthians. It is therefore striking that Mark does not put the phrase "in remembrance" there. The fact that it is here confirms Mark's intention to link this woman's gestures to the Eucharist. In preparing Jesus' body for burial, she has prepared his body for a death that will be life-giving. It is for her eucharistic gestures that she will be kept *"in remembrance."*

14:10-11 Preparation for betrayal continued

These two verses connect Judas with the plot to kill Jesus. They reintroduce the theme of betrayal. Mark consistently uses the phrase

Lesson Three

> [11] When they heard him they were pleased and promised to pay him money. Then he looked for an opportunity to hand him over.
>
> ### Preparations for the Passover
>
> [12] On the first day of the Feast of Unleavened Bread, when they sacrificed the Passover lamb, his disciples said to him, "Where do you want us to go and prepare for you to eat the Passover?" [13] He sent two of his disciples and said to them, "Go into the city and a man will meet you, carrying a jar of water. Follow him. [14] Wherever he enters, say to the master of the house, 'The Teacher says, "Where is my guest room where I may eat the Passover with my disciples?"' [15] Then he will show you a large upper room furnished and ready. Make the preparations for us there." [16] The disciples then went off, entered the city, and found it just as he had told them; and they prepared the Passover.
>
> ### The Betrayer
>
> [17] When it was evening, he came with the Twelve. [18] And as they reclined at table and were eating, Jesus said, "Amen, I say to you, one of you will betray me, one who is eating with me." [19] They began to be distressed and to say to him, one by one, "Surely it is not I?" [20] He said to them, "One of the Twelve, the one who dips with me into the dish. [21] For the Son of Man indeed goes, as it is written of him, but woe to that man by whom the Son of Man is betrayed. It would be better for that man if he had never been born."
>
> *continue*

institution of the Eucharist "on the night that he was *handed over*" (1 Cor 11:23).

14:12-16 Preparations for the Passover Supper

The details of this episode again seem both mysterious and symbolic, like the details of the anointing scene. Mark does not identify which disciples were sent or the man "carrying a jar of water" (14:13). Nor does he tell us how the man knows to lead the disciples to the right place. Mark also doesn't identify "the master of the house" nor tell us why he has already prepared a room for Jesus' Passover (14:14-15). The narrative's lack of realistic concreteness suggests that it is also intended to be symbolic.

In fact, many details suggest that Mark intends this narrative to symbolize the Eucharist. By referring to the Passover supper as "the Feast of Unleavened Bread" (v. 12), Mark stresses a detail that would be significant to a eucharistic community. When Mark notes that the disciples set off to prepare the supper on the day "when they sacrificed the Passover lamb" (14:12), he is calling attention to the sacrificial implications of the meal to come.

When Mark speaks of an anonymous man carrying a pottery water jar, the image seems to echo and complement the anonymous woman carrying an alabaster jar of costly ointment. We have noted that the alabaster jar indicates that it contains something precious and that the pouring out of its ointment anticipates Jesus' pouring out of the wine that he calls his blood. The pottery (or earthenware) jar is humble in comparison, and the water is ordinary compared with the precious ointment. One may think of Paul saying, "We hold this treasure in earthen vessels, that the surpassing power may be of God and not from us" (2 Cor 4:7). In any case, by presenting his readers with these different but echoing images, Mark suggests the pairing of water and wine that is part of the eucharistic celebration and proclaims, for the believer, the meeting of humanity with divinity.

In that context, the "large upper room furnished and ready" (14:15) is perhaps suggestive of the house churches that were developing

"hand over" to express betrayal. That use carries ironic overtones, because "hand over" can also mean *hand on*, as of a tradition. By his persistent repetition of the phrase, Mark suggests that Jesus is *handing on* the tradition of being *handed over*. It is the same word that Paul uses with the same double meaning when he says that he is *"handing on"* to the Christian community at Corinth what he knows about Jesus' in Mark's time to accommodate the eucharistic gatherings of the early Christian communities. Once again, Mark seems to be projecting his own time frame into the narrative. He is trying to give the reader his own awareness that this last Passover meal of Jesus was also the first Eucharist.

14:22-26 The Passover/Eucharist

In between predictions of betrayal, Mark places his account of the meal that he describes as both Passover and Eucharist. The blessing and breaking of bread, together with the blessing and giving of the cup (14:22-23), suggest the opening prayers of every Passover meal. (These read: "Blessed are you, O God, king of the universe, creator of the fruit of the vine.") It is also usual to conclude the Passover Seder, as they do here, with the singing of a hymn (14:26). What is strikingly different is Jesus' identification of the bread as his body and the wine as his blood (14:22-24). Mark also shows Jesus speaking of his blood as that "of the covenant" (14:24a). That reference suggests both the blood of the Passover lamb that saved the Israelites from destruction (Exod 12:13) and the sacrificial blood that ratified the covenant (Exod 24:8).

In addition, Mark shows Jesus quoting from Isaiah when he speaks of his blood being "shed for many" (14:24b). That phrase is also an echo of what Mark has shown Jesus saying earlier to his disciples about the purpose of his life: "For the Son of Man did not come to be served but to serve and to give his life as a ransom for many" (10:45). In both instances, the phrase is an echo of Isaiah's description of God's justification of his "Suffering Servant":

> Through his suffering, my servant shall justify many,
> and their guilt he shall bear (Isa 53:11; NAB).

By showing Jesus repeating this phrase, Mark interprets Jesus' death in that tradition of atoning sacrifice. It is also a tradition in which God raises up his servant and exalts him. Like the episode of Jesus' anointing, it is a suggestion of hope in this chapter so seemingly concentrated on betrayal and death.

The Lord's Supper

²²While they were eating, he took bread, said the blessing, broke it, and gave it to them, and said, "Take it; this is my body." ²³Then he took a cup, gave thanks, and gave it to them, and they all drank from it. ²⁴He said to them, "This is my blood of the covenant, which will be shed for many. ²⁵Amen, I say to you, I shall not drink again the fruit of the vine until the day when I drink it new in the kingdom of God." ²⁶Then, after singing a hymn, they went out to the Mount of Olives.

Peter's Denial Foretold

²⁷Then Jesus said to them, "All of you will have your faith shaken, for it is written:

'I will strike the shepherd,
and the sheep will be dispersed.'

²⁸But after I have been raised up, I shall go before you to Galilee." ²⁹Peter said to him, "Even though all should have their faith shaken, mine will not

continue

Another suggestion of hope is given in Jesus' further words that he will not drink "the fruit of the vine" again until the day when he drinks it new "in the kingdom of God" (14:25). Although in one sense it suggests that he is moving toward death, in another sense it offers hope that there will be another time, a new time, in which God's kingdom will at last prevail. And by showing that Jesus speaks of this time as one in which there will be "fruit of the vine" to drink, Mark also suggests that there will be a time when the fruit of God's vineyard will be accessible again to God.

14:17-21, 27-31 Predictions of betrayal

Mark frames the narrative of this Passover/Eucharist with predictions of Jesus' betrayal. The scene he describes before the supper (14:18) echoes a verse in Psalm 41 where the speaker recalls a time when friends as well as foes turned against him:

Lesson Three

be." ³⁰Then Jesus said to him, "Amen, I say to you, this very night before the cock crows twice you will deny me three times." ³¹But he vehemently replied, "Even though I should have to die with you, I will not deny you." And they all spoke similarly.

The Agony in the Garden

³²Then they came to a place named Gethsemane, and he said to his disciples, "Sit here while I pray." ³³He took with him Peter, James, and John, and began to be troubled and distressed. ³⁴Then he said to them, "My soul is sorrowful even to death. Remain here and keep watch." ³⁵He advanced a little and fell to the ground and prayed that if it were possible the hour might pass by him; ³⁶he said, "Abba, Father, all things are possible to you. Take this cup away from me, but not what I will but what you will." ³⁷When he returned he found them asleep. He said to Peter, "Simon, are you asleep? Could you not keep watch for one hour? ³⁸Watch and pray that you may not undergo the test. The spirit is willing but the flesh is weak." ³⁹Withdrawing again, he prayed, saying the same thing. ⁴⁰Then he returned once more and found them asleep, for they could not keep their eyes

continue

Even my trusted friend,
 who ate my bread,
  has raised his heel against me (v. 10).

When Mark then shows Jesus saying that his betrayer will be "the one who dips with me into the dish" (14:20), he brings to mind both the dipping gesture characteristic of the Passover Seder and the dipping posture of baptism. By suggesting both simultaneously, Mark suggests that the experience of being betrayed is the tradition of God's servants. (Being *handed over* is being *handed on*).

When Mark shows Jesus saying, "For the Son of Man indeed goes, as it is written of him" (14:21), he indicates how much his narrative uses Scripture to shape and interpret the story of Jesus' passion. The foretelling of the disciples' betrayal (14:27) is preceded by a passage from Zechariah:

[I will] strike the shepherd
 that the sheep may be scattered (Zech 13:7).

In the context of Zechariah, God is saying that he will strike the shepherd *so that* the sheep may be dispersed. God says that he will purge Israel of false prophets and false shepherds so that he can preserve the remnant and make Jerusalem holy again. In Mark, the prophecy is used to indicate how all the Twelve, including Peter, will scatter and leave Jesus without their support.

When Mark shows Jesus making this prediction to Peter, it is even more precise: "Amen, I say to you, this very night before the cock crows twice you will deny me three times" (14:30). Mark thus links Jesus' warning to Peter to his general admonition to "watchfulness" in chapter 13: "You do not know when the lord of the house is coming, whether in the evening, or at midnight, or at cockcrow . . ." (13:35). The vehemence of Peter's refusal to accept himself as a possible betrayer (14:29, 31) intensifies the enormity of his eventual act of betrayal (14:66-72).

Yet even in this context of betrayal, Mark shows Jesus predicting once again that he will be raised from the dead (14:28). In this instance, Mark shows him speaking not only about his being raised but about his life beyond death: "I shall go before you to Galilee." It is striking because his words do not suggest ascension to heaven (like Elijah), but a return to ongoing ministry. And this phrase is the one the women at the tomb are sent to repeat to the disciples after Jesus' death (16:7).

14:32-52 Betrayal in the garden
This betrayal has two parts: (1) betrayal by the three key disciples (14:32-42), and (2) betrayal by Judas (14:43-52).

14:32-42 Betrayal by the disciples. The first part is conventionally labeled "Agony in the Garden," although in fact there is no explicit

Wm Barber - moral Mondays

mention of a garden; the garden setting is inferred from knowledge of Gethsemane. The image of betrayal in a garden fits in with the fact that Creation provides Mark's overall frame of reference. In that context, there is particular irony in Mark showing Jesus, second Adam, betrayed in a garden.

There is also irony within the scene itself. We have noted before that Mark shows Jesus taking these same three disciples with him at three key moments in the Gospel: at the raising up of Jairus's daughter (5:37); at the transfiguration of Jesus (9:2); and here. The first two episodes point toward Jesus' resurrection. In fact, in terms of the overall structure of Mark's narrative, the transfiguration scene takes the place of a resurrection scene. In this scene in the garden, all the elements of the transfiguration scene are reversed. Mark tells us that instead of being radiant and dazzling (9:3), Jesus is "troubled and distressed" (14:33). Instead of ascending up a mountain (9:2), Jesus falls to the ground (14:35). Instead of being blessed by the Father (9:7), Jesus cries out to the Father to take away his coming suffering and death (14:36). Peter, who is so roused by the moment of transfiguration that he wants to celebrate it (9:5), falls asleep (14:37). It is also significant that Mark shows Jesus not addressing him here as "Peter" but reverting to "Simon," the name he had before he became a disciple.

Mark connects this scene to others in his Gospel as well. By showing that Jesus refers to his suffering as "this cup," Mark links this scene to Jesus' question to James and John: "Can you drink the cup that I drink . . . ?" (10:38). The word is, of course, also linked to the Passover/Eucharist Mark has just described and to the cup of Jesus' blood (14:23-24).

By showing that Jesus cries out "Abba," the Aramaic word for "father" (14:36), Mark indicates the importance of this moment. He shows Jesus using Aramaic only in three other key places: when Jesus raises up the little girl from death (5:41); when Jesus symbolically heals the deaf-mute (7:34); and when Jesus cries out to God from the cross (15:34).

> open and did not know what to answer him. [41]He returned a third time and said to them, "Are you still sleeping and taking your rest? It is enough. The hour has come. Behold, the Son of Man is to be handed over to sinners. [42]Get up, let us go. See, my betrayer is at hand."
>
> ### The Betrayal and Arrest of Jesus
>
> [43]Then, while he was still speaking, Judas, one of the Twelve, arrived, accompanied by a crowd with swords and clubs who had come from the chief priests, the scribes, and the elders. [44]His betrayer had arranged a signal with them, saying, "The man I shall kiss is the one; arrest him and lead him away securely." [45]He came and immediately
>
> *continue*

Most important, Mark shows Jesus using the word "watch" three times in this brief episode (14:34, 37, 38). Like the "cockcrow" (14:30), this refrain links this moment to the warnings at the end of chapter 13 (13:33, 35, 37). There, at the conclusion of the parable of the returning lord of the house, Jesus says to his disciples, "May he not come suddenly and find you sleeping. What I say to you, I say to all: 'Watch!'" (13:36-37). Here Jesus comes back to his disciples three times and finds them asleep.

Jesus' announcement that "the Son of Man is to be handed over to sinners" (14:41b) picks up the theme of being "handed over." It is full of irony in view of the fact that throughout the Gospel Mark has shown Jesus reaching out to sinners.

The phrase translated above as "Get up!" (14:42) is literally "You are raised up!"* It is again ironic. By means of it, Mark indicates the distance between what the disciples ought to be and what in fact they are.

14:43-52 Betrayal by Judas. The betrayal by Judas follows upon the more subtle betrayals by the three key disciples. It is signaled by

Lesson Three

> went over to him and said, "Rabbi." And he kissed him. ⁴⁶At this they laid hands on him and arrested him. ⁴⁷One of the bystanders drew his sword, struck the high priest's servant, and cut off his ear. ⁴⁸Jesus said to them in reply, "Have you come out as against a robber, with swords and clubs, to seize me? ⁴⁹Day after day I was with you teaching in the temple area, yet you did not arrest me; but that the scriptures may be fulfilled." ⁵⁰And they all left him and fled. ⁵¹Now a young man followed him wearing nothing but a linen cloth about his body. They seized him, ⁵²but he left the cloth behind and ran off naked.
>
> *continue*

Mark's word for moral urgency, "straightway"* (omitted in the translation given here for 14:43). Judas comes as the agent of the Temple authorities—"the chief priests, the scribes, and the elders" (14:43). The crowd that accompanies him is the reverse of "the crowd" we have seen earlier that follows after Jesus. The "sign" that Judas has arranged with them (14:44) is doubly ironic. It is ironic because of the earlier episode where the Pharisees sought "a sign from heaven" (8:11). It is ironic because the sign of betrayal is a kiss (14:44).

Mark's irony continues as he says that Judas approached Jesus "straightway" (again translated as "immediately" above) and addressed him by the honorific "Rabbi" before he kissed him (14:45).

When Mark goes on to say, "they laid hands on him and arrested him" (14:46), the reader hears an ironic echo of Jesus' "laying his hands" on the sick to cure them (6:5).

When Mark shows Jesus asking, "Have you come out as against a robber?" (14:48), the reader hears an ironic echo of Jeremiah's sermon that reproaches the Temple authorities for turning the Temple into "a den of thieves" (11:17).

The reference to the fulfillment of the Scriptures (14:49) should be understood in terms of the passage from Zechariah quoted earlier in this chapter (14:27):

> [I will] strike the shepherd,
>   that the sheep may be scattered.

Mark shows its fulfillment here by the terse statement "And they all left him and fled" (14:50).

The episode concludes with Mark's description of a young man who started to follow Jesus until the crowd seized hold of him; then he left behind the linen cloth on his body "and ran off naked" (14:51-52). The incident dramatizes the kind of situation warned about earlier in 13:14-16: "When you see the desolating abomination . . . a person in a field must not return to get his cloak." By this dramatic image, Mark suggests that the "tribulation" warned about in chapter 13 has begun.

The **unnamed young follower** of Jesus who appears in this climactic scene is not an accidental figure. In such a compact Gospel as that of Mark, there is little room for incidentals. But what does he bring to the story? What does he represent to the reader? Those present at the arrest of Jesus included not only those followers we have come to know by name but also some whose identities are never known. Jesus touched many who apparently followed him without fanfare. It happened then and it happens now. What are we to make of the simple linen cloth worn by this man? Is this a literary technique included only to give drama to the story, or is it intended to prefigure the linen cloth that will wrap Jesus in death? Does he leave it behind in personal terror or does he leave it behind in anticipation of Jesus' eventual need for it? And what are we to make of the young man running off? The scene is somewhat reminiscent of the rich man who went away sad when told that to inherit eternal life he is to sell all his possessions (10:17-22). Is this young follower who literally left everything behind as he departed an intentional "counter-reminder" of that rich man whose fate we never know? Is the young man at least to be praised for staying on the scene longer than the named disciples of Jesus who fled immediately? Discipleship requires everything of us: following without recognition or fanfare, being present with Jesus and his followers even in the dark hours, simplicity of life, and the willingness to stay the course rather than flee the unexpected.

Summary of the passion narrative, Part I (14:1-52)

Part I of the passion narrative interweaves two contrasting themes, one of which leads to death and the other to life. The episodes of the chapter show preparations being made for both.

The negative theme, that of betrayal, appears to dominate. The chapter opens with chief priests and scribes plotting to kill Jesus, and it concludes with his arrest in the garden. In the middle verses, Mark shows Judas joining the conspiracy to kill Jesus. Mark's account of the Last Supper is framed by Jesus' predictions of the betrayals by Judas and Peter. The scene in the garden reverses all the elements of the transfiguration: Jesus "falls to the ground," while the three key disciples—Peter, James, and John—fail to "watch" with him. After Jesus' arrest, all his disciples desert him. From the point of view of plot, the preparation for Jesus' death appears to be advancing inevitably.

Yet, interwoven into this death-leading plot are events that suggest Jesus' continued life in the Eucharist. First, Mark tells us of an anonymous woman who anoints Jesus for his death. Mark describes her gestures in such a way that they anticipate the Eucharist. The Eucharist is further symbolized by the pairing of this anonymous woman with her alabaster vase of ointment and the anonymous man with his earthenware jar of water. The woman "shatters" the vase and "pours out" the precious ointment. Her extravagant gestures prepare for Jesus' extravagant gestures of breaking and pouring out. The anonymous man with his earthen vessel leads Jesus' disciples to a large room already prepared to receive them. Together, they suggest the early eucharistic communities meeting in house churches and reliving Jesus' gestures "in remembrance" of him.

These episodes introduce the description of the Passover meal in which Jesus speaks of the bread as his body and the wine as his blood. In its introductory blessings and its final hymn, it is a traditional Passover meal, celebrating God's act of freeing his people from slavery. In the midst of this traditional framework, Jesus speaks of his body as the bread to be broken and of the wine as his blood to be "shed for

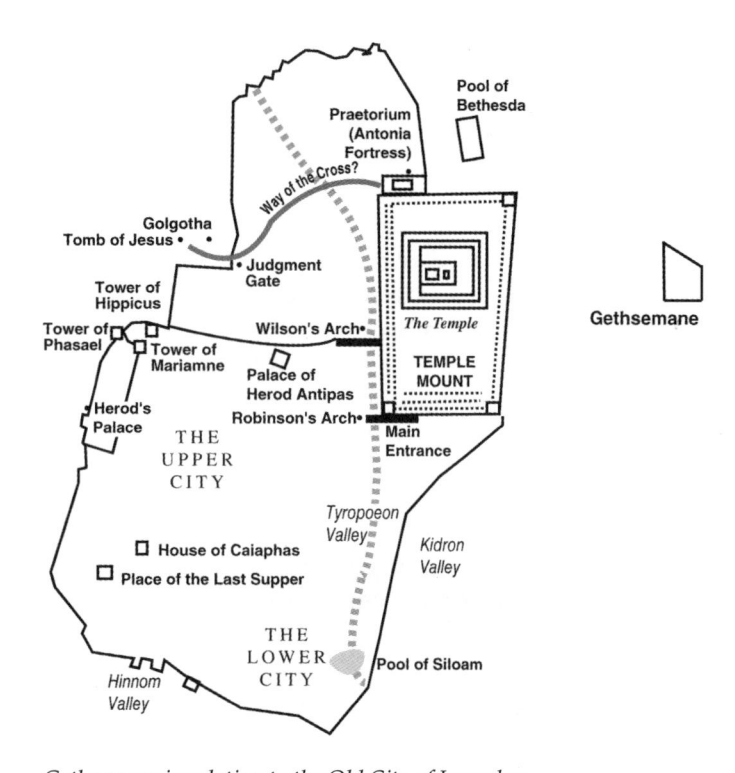

Gethsemane in relation to the Old City of Jerusalem

Lesson Three

> ### Jesus before the Sanhedrin
>
> ⁵³They led Jesus away to the high priest, and all the chief priests and the elders and the scribes came together. ⁵⁴Peter followed him at a distance into the high priest's courtyard and was seated with the guards, warming himself at the fire. ⁵⁵The chief priests and the entire Sanhedrin kept trying to obtain testimony against Jesus in order to put him to death, but they found none. ⁵⁶Many gave false witness against him, but their testimony did not agree. ⁵⁷Some took the stand and testified falsely against him, alleging, ⁵⁸"We heard him say,
>
> *continue*

many." In this way he links his blood to the saving blood of the covenant and to the atoning blood of Isaiah's Suffering Servant. He reverses the effect of the vineyard parable by predicting a future day when the vineyard's fruit will again be accessible and God's kingdom will prevail. His words imply the paradox of a death that will be life-giving. After the supper, even while he is predicting the scattering of his disciples, he speaks of his life beyond death.

In Mark's telling of it, Part I of the passion narrative presents episodes and scriptural echoes that prepare simultaneously for Jesus' death and for his new life. The plot seems to be moving inevitably toward his death, but the framework of Passover freedom, together with hints of the kingdom to come, life beyond death in Galilee, and a eucharistic community holding him "in remembrance," points to a dramatic irony in which what looks like the end may in fact be a new beginning.

THE PASSION NARRATIVE, PART II: THE IDENTITY OF JESUS ON TRIAL

Mark 14:53–15:15

14:53-65 Jesus before the high priest

As we read this account, it is important to remember the place of the high priest in Judaism at the time of Jesus. As we explained earlier, the high priest at this time was appointed by the Romans and did not represent the religious leadership of the Jews. The "chief priests and the elders and the scribes" who accompany the high priest here (14:53) should also be understood as part of a group that were collaborating with Rome. Their plot to kill Jesus, therefore, together with their questions and their response to him, must be seen in this context. (Mark has earlier shown Jesus' total agreement with a different sort of scribe in 12:28-34.)

Mark establishes the injustice of the trial by noting that from the outset "the chief priests and the entire Sanhedrin kept trying to obtain testimony against Jesus in order to put him to death, but they found none" (14:55). Mark notes that not having found any valid evidence against Jesus, they offered "false witness" (14:56a). This testimony is further invalidated by the fact that the witnesses did not agree (14:56b, 59). (Having at least two witnesses who agree is a requirement of Deuteronomy 19:15.) The false witness that they offer has to do with the Temple: "We heard him say, 'I will destroy this temple made with hands and within three days I will build another not made with hands'" (14:58). Mark has earlier given the reader an account of what Jesus said about the Temple (ch. 13), so the reader can judge how false this statement is.

Of course, the reader familiar with the interpretation given in John—"But he was speaking about the temple of his body" (John 2:21)—may read this false accusation as containing an ironic truth, but within the framework of Mark's Gospel, Jesus has spoken only of the Temple being destroyed (13:2). Yet the reader who knows the end of the story may be haunted anyway by the ironic mixture here of uncanny truth with deliberate falsehood.

The questions of the high priest also have ironic elements. When the high priest asks, "Are you [the Anointed One] the Messiah, the son of the Blessed One?" (14:61), he is asking the key questions of Mark's narrative about Jesus' identity. Mark has earlier shown Jesus reproving Peter for identifying him as a triumphant, non-suffering messiah (8:33). Mark has just shown Jesus becoming "the Anointed One" in the context of death (14:8). He has also just shown that for Jesus, the implication of being "the son of the Blessed One" is acceptance of the Father's will, even to the point of death (14:36).

Jesus' response here, however, does not stress his death but his glory. Mark shows him quoting Daniel 7:13 when he describes himself as "Son of Man . . . coming with the clouds of heaven." In Daniel's context, the phrase describes an angelic figure who comes in human form ("One *like* a son of man") and who represents the people of God in contrast to worldly kingdoms, described as beasts. We have noted before that Mark shows Jesus applying this phrase to himself as a way of indicating that he represents all humanity. Mark uses the phrase to suggest that Jesus is a second Adam, giving all of us a second chance.

Mark shows Jesus adding to that reference the image of himself "seated at the right hand of the Power" (14:62). The image of someone seated "at the right hand" of God comes from the first verse of Psalm 110, where God is reassuring his anointed king that he will protect him from his enemies:

> The LORD says to my lord:
> "Take your throne at my right hand,
> while I make your enemies your footstool."

In chapter 12, Mark has shown Jesus quoting this psalm in order to raise questions about the nature of the Messiah or Anointed One (12:35-37). Here Mark shows Jesus implicitly identifying himself with this figure. Yet Mark has also shown, through Jesus' rebuke of Peter (8:33), that Jesus defines "messiah" differently from those who associate the term with triumphant power in this world.

Mark shows the high priest responding in a way that reveals he does not share Jesus' understanding of the terms "messiah" or "son of the Blessed One." The high priest responds by tearing his garments and calling Jesus' reply

---

> 'I will destroy this temple made with hands and within three days I will build another not made with hands.'" ⁵⁹Even so their testimony did not agree. ⁶⁰The high priest rose before the assembly and questioned Jesus, saying, "Have you no answer? What are these men testifying against you?" ⁶¹But he was silent and answered nothing. Again the high priest asked him and said to him, "Are you the Messiah, the son of the Blessed One?" ⁶²Then Jesus answered, "I am; and
>
> > 'you will see the Son of Man
> > seated at the right hand of the Power
> > and coming with the clouds of heaven.'"
>
> ⁶³At that the high priest tore his garments and said, "What further need have we of witnesses? ⁶⁴You have heard the blasphemy. What do you think?" They all condemned him as deserving to die. ⁶⁵Some began to spit on him. They blindfolded him and struck him and said to him, "Prophesy!" And the guards greeted him with blows.
>
> *continue*

---

a "blasphemy" (14:64). The high priest implies that it is blasphemous to refer to oneself by either of these terms. But in Jewish law, that was not the case. "Blasphemy" is defined in Leviticus as "cursing" God (Lev 24:15-16), not anything else. Being called "messiah" means being called the one anointed to do God's work; it is hardly a term hostile to God. And being "son of God" was a claim that any pious Jew might make. By this reply, Mark shows the high priest to be either ignorant of Jewish law and custom or indifferent to it. Mark is thus dramatizing the fact that the high priest of that time was not a religious leader but a worldly one. In league with Rome, he did not know or care about Jewish piety.

In addition, Mark constructs the scene of Jesus' trial by interweaving echoes of Scripture that reveal how much it is the pattern for God's just one to be misunderstood and condemned by the powers of the world. First of all, Mark

Lesson Three

> **Peter's Denial of Jesus**
>
> ⁶⁶While Peter was below in the courtyard, one of the high priest's maids came along. ⁶⁷Seeing Peter warming himself, she looked intently at him and said, "You too were with the Nazarene, Jesus." ⁶⁸But he denied it saying, "I neither know nor understand what you are talking about." So he went out into the outer court. [Then the cock crowed.] ⁶⁹The maid saw him and began again to say to the bystanders, "This man is one of them." ⁷⁰Once again he denied it. A little later the bystanders said to Peter once more, "Surely you are one of them; for you too are a Galilean." ⁷¹He began to curse and to swear, "I do not know this man about whom you are talking." ⁷²And immediately a cock crowed a second time. Then Peter remembered the word that Jesus had said to him, "Before the cock crows twice you will deny me three times." He broke down and wept.

seems to be reenacting the scene in the Wisdom of Solomon where "the wicked" set out to "lie in wait for the righteous one" (Wis 2:12) because "he professes to have knowledge of God and styles himself a child of the LORD" (Wis 2:13) and "boasts that God is his Father" (Wis 2:16b). The "wicked" in the Wisdom of Solomon also go on to condemn the just man "to a shameful death" (Wis 2:20).

Second, by saying that "Some began to spit on him" and "struck him" (14:65), Mark seems also to be summoning up the third song of Isaiah's "Suffering Servant" figure:

> I gave my back to those who beat me,
>   my cheeks to those who tore out my beard;
> My face I did not hide
>   from insults and spitting (Isa 50:6).

Like "the just one" of the Wisdom of Solomon, the Suffering Servant is mocked and condemned by the obtuse powers of the world, who do not understand his identity as God's servant. By echoing both those works, Mark is providing an interpretive framework for understanding the condemnation and death of Jesus.

The **Sanhedrin** (from the Greek *synedrion*, meaning "seat") appears to have emerged as a governing body for the Jewish people sometime after the exile (6th century B.C.E.). The power the Sanhedrin wielded varied according to the prevailing political situation. At the time of Jesus, the Sanhedrin in Jerusalem—composed of priests, elders, scribes, and Pharisees, and led by a high priest—had authority to settle religious issues in Judea and interacted with Roman officials in some secular matters as well. The number of members who were part of the Sanhedrin is often given as seventy (excluding the high priest), which matches the number of elders who accompanied Moses up Mount Sinai to ratify the covenant (Exod 24:1, 9).

14:66-72 Peter denies knowing Jesus

Mark shows the two trials to be about Jesus' identity. He bridges these two trials with the episode in which Jesus' key disciple denies knowing who Jesus is. Peter's presence "in the courtyard" (14:66) picks up an earlier point in Mark's narrative (14:54). The structure is the typical Markan "sandwich" we have noted before, for example in Mark's placement of the story of John the Baptist's death (6:17-29) and in his narrative of the healing of the woman with a menstrual disorder (5:25-34). In each instance, the middle section sheds light on the parts it separates. So here the episode of Peter's denial of Jesus illuminates the trials that center on Jesus' identity.

Both the high priest and Pilate condemn Jesus by misrepresenting his identity as one that claims power. They both function as false witnesses to Jesus. At the other extreme, Mark shows Peter refusing to witness at all.

Ironically, one of the high priest's maids bears witness to Peter's identity ("You too were with the Nazarene, Jesus," 14:67b). This identification of Peter is repeated two more times (14:69-70). Mark creates a triad of true identifications of Peter that balance the triad, under Pilate, of false identifications of Jesus. Peter's denials are incrementally more vehement. The narrative reaches its climax when the cock crows a second time (14:72) and Peter remembers the prediction of Jesus, "Amen, I say to you, this very night before the cock crows twice, you will deny me three times" (14:30). The second cockcrow is prefaced by the key word "straightway"* (translated above as "immediately"). Mark notes that upon hearing it, Peter "broke down and wept" (14:72b). Mark is dramatizing the fact that in denying Jesus, Peter has been denying himself. In Mark's account, Peter's identity is bound to the identity of Jesus. Ironically, too, Peter's denial of himself is not the kind of self-denial that Jesus asked of his followers (8:34). Rather, Mark shows it is the opposite: Peter denies knowing Jesus because he is trying to save himself from a similar fate. Mark's narrative dramatizes the truth of Jesus' wisdom: "Whoever wishes to save his life will lose it" (8:35). The other side of that truth remains for now only in the reader's mind.

Lesson Three

EXPLORING LESSON THREE

1. a) When Jesus' disciples ask him about "the end," what does he indicate are not necessarily signs of "the end" (13:3-13)?

    b) What must happen first before "the end" (13:10)?

2. What are some ways we can maintain watchfulness even if there is no certainty of when Jesus will return (13:32-36)?

3. Jesus tells his disciples, "The poor you will always have with you" (14:7). Why should this not be interpreted to mean we can ignore their plight? (See 14:3-9; 10:21; and Deut 15:11, 16.)

4. Explain the Jewish concept behind the words "in memory" found in 14:9 and spoken in the words of consecration at each Mass.

Lesson Three

5. What elements of Jesus' celebration of the Passover are recorded by Mark in such a way that they can clearly be associated with the Eucharist (14:12, 22-25)?

6. What Old Testament connections can be made with Jesus identifying one of the Passover cups with "my blood of the covenant" (14:23-24)? (See Exod 12:2-7; 24:6-8.)

7. When have you needed someone's company in a time of great stress, fear, or grief (14:32-42)? If you had someone accompany you in such a time, what difference did it make for you?

8. How is Peter's denial of Jesus different from Judas's denial? (See 14:43-47, 66-72.)

9. Write about your memories of attending Holy Thursday and Good Friday services. What do these celebrations mean to you?

CLOSING PRAYER

Prayer

And immediately a cock crowed a second time. Then Peter remembered the word that Jesus had said to him, "Before the cock crows twice you will deny me three times." He broke down and wept.

(Mark 14:72)

Gentle Jesus, how often we deny you by failing to lead lives of charity, compassion, and service! Help us to be like Peter, to have true contrition when we turn away from you. Today we especially pray for the grace to . . .

LESSON FOUR

Mark 15–16

Begin your personal study and group discussion with a simple and sincere prayer such as:

Prayer

Lord Jesus, as we read this Gospel, may we hear your words and meditate on your life with open hearts and alert minds. May our time of study and sharing strengthen our faith in you, the source of all truth and wisdom.

Read the Bible text of Mark 15–16 found in the outside columns of pages 68–85, highlighting what stands out to you.

Read the accompanying commentary to add to your understanding.

Respond to the questions on pages 87–88, Exploring Lesson Four.

The Closing Prayer on page 89 is for your personal use and may be used at the end of group discussion.

Lesson Four

CHAPTER 15

Jesus before Pilate

¹As soon as morning came, the chief priests with the elders and the scribes, that is, the whole Sanhedrin, held a council. They bound Jesus, led him away, and handed him over to Pilate. ²Pilate questioned him, "Are you the king of the Jews?" He said to him in reply, "You say so." ³The chief priests accused him of many things. ⁴Again Pilate questioned him, "Have you no answer? See how many things they accuse you of." ⁵Jesus gave him no further answer, so that Pilate was amazed.

continue

15:1-15 Jesus before Pilate

As we have seen, Mark shows the high priest falsely accusing Jesus of blasphemy. His accusation serves to reveal both his ignorance of Jewish religious law and his underlying fear of Jesus' power. Mark shows that he does not understand the terms "messiah" and "son of the Blessed" in a spiritual sense but sees them as a threat to his worldly power. Mark emphasizes the concern of the high priest for worldly power by structuring Jesus' trial before Pilate as a parallel to it. In both instances, Mark shows that the one interrogating Jesus is not interested in what Jesus has done but in who he is and how his identity may threaten their own.

Mark shows Pilate's main concern to be whether Jesus considers himself "the king of the Jews." In Mark's account, Pilate repeats this phrase three times, like a refrain. The first time, Pilate asks the question directly of Jesus (15:2). The second time, he uses the term in a question to the crowd: "Do you want me to release to you the king of the Jews?" (15:9). The third time, Pilate uses it to address the crowd about Jesus' fate: "Then what [do you want] me to do with [the man you call] the king of the Jews?" (15:12).

To grasp the full effect of this refrain, it is helpful for the modern reader to know that the term was in fact a title that the Romans applied to their designated tetrarchs. At the time of Jesus, Herod Antipas was tetrarch of Galilee, while Judea was directly under the administration of Roman procurators like Pilate. Needless to say, ordinary Jews of the time did not like the idea of a Roman appointee being called their "king." Pilate's reference to Jesus by this term was therefore politically charged. By showing Pilate's repeated use of it, Mark indicates that Pilate fired up the crowd to think that Jesus either was a tool of Rome or had claimed such an alliance for himself. While on the surface Mark's narrative seems to suggest that Pilate turned over Jesus' fate to the Jewish crowd, at a more subtle level Mark is showing how Pilate incited the crowd to anger.

Just as Mark shows the high priest trying to turn the religious community against Jesus on the false claim that he had committed some kind of blasphemy, so he shows Pilate trying to turn the crowds against Jesus on the false claim that he had taken to himself a title of Roman power.

The scene has other ironic details worth noting. In the opening verse, Mark says that "the chief priests with the elders and the scribes" held a council about Jesus *"straightway"** (a word omitted in the translation above). Mark repeats the key word of the theme of betrayal by saying they *"handed him* *over* to Pilate" (15:1b, emphasis added). The word for "release," which Mark has associated before with Jesus' acts of freeing people from physical ailments or from sin, appears here in the question of Pilate: "Do you want me to release to you the king of the Jews?" (15:9). This question is the middle one of the triad of references to Jesus as "the king of the Jews," thus stressing its irony.

Pontius Pilate was the Roman procurator of Judea from 25 to 35 C.E. Procurators were officers assigned to oversee the administration of provinces within the empire and usually reported to a governor of a larger region. Historical accounts of Pilate paint an unflattering picture of his character, describing him as excessively cruel and given to violence and corruption. Over the centuries many legends developed concerning Pilate in the Christian community. Some of these narratives tell of his origins and detail the assorted crimes he allegedly committed both before and after Jesus' passion, while others recount his death (which was generally ascribed to suicide).

Summary of the passion narrative, Part II (14:53–15:15)

Part II of Mark's passion narrative focuses on the identity of Jesus. There are two balancing scenes in which the identity of Jesus is put on trial. Each trial is characterized by a falsification of who Jesus is; in each case, Jesus is condemned on false grounds. In the trial before the high priest, Jesus is condemned as a blasphemer, although he has said nothing that would constitute blasphemy according to Jewish law. In the trial before Pilate, Jesus is condemned as a would-be "king of the Jews," although he had never claimed that Roman title or sought that Roman power.

In between these matching trials and false witnesses, Mark gives an account of Peter's refusal to witness to Jesus at all. As Mark tells

The Sentence of Death

⁶Now on the occasion of the feast he used to release to them one prisoner whom they requested. ⁷A man called Barabbas was then in prison along with the rebels who had committed murder in a rebellion. ⁸The crowd came forward and began to ask him to do for them as he was accustomed. ⁹Pilate answered, "Do you want me to release to you the king of the Jews?" ¹⁰For he knew that it was out of envy that the chief priests had handed him over. ¹¹But the chief priests stirred up the crowd to have him release Barabbas for them instead. ¹²Pilate again said to them in reply, "Then what [do you want] me to do with [the man you call] the king of the Jews?" ¹³They shouted again, "Crucify him." ¹⁴Pilate said to them, "Why? What evil has he done?" They only shouted the louder, "Crucify him." ¹⁵So Pilate, wishing to satisfy the crowd, released Barabbas to them and, after he had Jesus scourged, handed him over to be crucified.

continue

the story, Peter's denial of Jesus is also a denial of himself.

In Mark's narrative, the high priest, Pilate, and Peter are alike in trying to save themselves. As a consequence, each one betrays himself: the high priest betrays that he is not truly a religious leader of the Jews; Pilate betrays that he is not truly an administrator of justice; Peter betrays that he is not truly a disciple of Jesus. Their false witness to Jesus is pivotal to their own identities.

THE PASSION NARRATIVE, PART III: THE DEATH OF JESUS

Mark 15:6-47

15:6 The death sentence

We have already suggested that Mark shows Pilate inciting the crowd by referring to Jesus repeatedly as "the king of the Jews" (15:2, 9, 12).

Lesson Four

> ### Mockery by the Soldiers
>
> ¹⁶The soldiers led him away inside the palace, that is, the praetorium, and assembled the whole cohort. ¹⁷They clothed him in purple and, weaving a crown of thorns, placed it on him. ¹⁸They began to salute him with, "Hail, King of the Jews!" ¹⁹and kept striking his head with a reed and spitting upon him. They knelt before him in homage. ²⁰And when they had mocked him, they stripped him of the purple cloak, dressed him in his own clothes, and led him out to crucify him.
>
> ### The Way of the Cross
>
> ²¹They pressed into service a passer-by, Simon, a Cyrenian, who was coming in from the country, the father of Alexander and Rufus, to carry his cross.
>
> *continue*

Mark tells the story of the death sentence in such a way that everyone is implicated: the crowd that shouts "Crucify him" (15:13-14); the chief priests, who have stirred them up to this (15:11); and Pilate, who, "wishing to satisfy the crowd" (15:15), handed Jesus over to be crucified. Although Mark reports the involvement of the crowd, he shapes the narrative to place the greatest blame on the chief priests and Pilate—that is, the agents of Rome. In particular, he indicates the moral weakness of Pilate by showing that he knows Jesus is innocent (15:14) and nonetheless condemns him, just "to satisfy the crowd" (15:15).

15:16-20 The mockery of Jesus

In this description of the Roman soldiers' mockery of Jesus, Mark dramatizes the irony of calling Jesus "king of the Jews" (15:18). He expands upon the image of Isaiah's "Suffering Servant," to which he had alluded earlier (14:65):

> I gave my back to those who beat me,
>   my cheeks to those who tore out my beard;
> My face I did not hide
>   from insults and spitting (Isa 50:6).

Here the "buffets and spitting" accompany the elaborate mockery of the purple cloak and crown of thorns (15:17), the mocking salutation (15:18), and posture of kneeling (15:19).

The whole scene also expands upon the brief suggestion in the Wisdom of Solomon of "the wicked" torturing "the just one":

> With violence and torture let us put him to the test
>   that we may have proof of his gentleness
>   and try his patience.
> Let us condemn him to a shameful death;
>   for according to his own words, God will take care of him (Wis 2:19-20).

The mock homage also ironically recalls three earlier instances in Mark's Gospel where some knelt in all seriousness before Jesus: the leper seeking to be healed (1:40); the demons who recognized him as "son of God" (3:11);

But in fact, Mark is more precise than that. He indicates that Pilate used that title to arouse the chief priests, because "he knew that it was out of envy that the chief priests had handed him over" (15:10). After that, Mark says, "the chief priests stirred up the crowd to have him release Barabbas for them instead" (15:11).

The release of Barabbas is further Markan irony. It is ironic from the point of view of the Roman trial because Barabbas, Mark tells us, is a known insurgent against Rome and a murderer as well (15:7). And it is ironic from the point of view of the Jewish trial because the name Barabbas means in Hebrew "son of the Father." Jesus, who has no plans to strike against Rome, is put to death, while a convicted rebel against Rome is released. Jesus is condemned for calling himself "son of the Blessed," while one whose very name means the same thing is released.

The word "released" is also used by Mark as an ironic refrain, being repeated three times in this short episode (15:9, 11, 15). The theme that Mark has repeatedly associated with Jesus' acts of forgiveness and healing is repeatedly used here in connection with Jesus' sentence of death.

and the woman who touched him and was overwhelmed by her cure (5:33).

15:21 Simon forced to take up the cross

The reappearance of the name "Simon" here has symbolic significance. Mark has just shown us Simon Peter denying Jesus while refusing to "deny himself and take up his cross." (The language of denial here explicitly repeats the language of 8:34.) Like Simon the leper, this Simon also functions as his alter ego, forced into doing what Simon Peter the disciple has not been able to do.

The other names in this brief incident are significant as well. "Simon" was a Jewish name, and Cyrene was apparently a Greek colony where many Jews had settled. The names "Alexander" and "Rufus" are, respectively, Greek and Roman. Through these names, Mark suggests how Jesus' followers were eventually to include the Greek and the Roman world.

Archaeologists have identified the site of the Church of the Holy Sepulchre in the heart of the Old City of Jerusalem as the most likely location of **Golgotha**. Since ancient times, Christians have revered the site as the place of Jesus' burial, despite some scholarly proposals that locate Jesus' tomb elsewhere. In Jesus' day, Golgotha was a quarry outside the city walls.

15:22-32 Crucifixion

Mark translates the name "Golgotha" as "Place of the Skull." His Jewish audience would have known the legend that it was the burial place of Adam's skull. Thus even as he shows Jesus being led to his death, Mark calls attention to the fact that Jesus is a second Adam. Mark thus suggests the cosmic irony of his death.

The "wine drugged with myrrh" (15:23) echoes the distress expressed by the psalmist, who says "I have become an outcast to my kindred" because "zeal for your house has consumed me" (Ps 69:9-10). In his anguish, he cries out:

The Crucifixion

²²They brought him to the place of Golgotha (which is translated Place of the Skull). ²³They gave him wine drugged with myrrh, but he did not take it. ²⁴Then they crucified him and divided his garments by casting lots for them to see what each should take. ²⁵It was nine o'clock in the morning when they crucified him. ²⁶The inscription of the charge against him read, "The King of the Jews." ²⁷With him they crucified two revolutionaries, one on his right and one on his left. [²⁸] ²⁹Those passing by reviled him, shaking their heads and saying, "Aha! You who would destroy the temple and rebuild it in three days, ³⁰save yourself by coming down from the cross." ³¹Likewise the chief priests, with the scribes, mocked him among themselves and said, "He saved others; he cannot save himself. ³²Let the Messiah, the King of Israel, come down now from the cross that we may see and believe." Those who were crucified with him also kept abusing him.

continue

Insult has broken my heart, and I despair.
  I looked for compassion, but there was none,
  for comforters, but found none.
Instead, they gave me poison for my food;
  and for my thirst they gave me vinegar (Ps 69:21-22).

Similarly, the detail about the soldiers' dividing Jesus' clothes (15:24) recalls the agony of the innocent one in Psalm 22:

They stare at me and gloat;
  they divide my garments among them;
  for my clothing they cast lots (Ps 22:18b-19).

The passers-by who shake their heads at Jesus (15:29), along with their mocking taunts to "save yourself" (15:30), also recall Psalm 22:

All who see me mock me;
  they curl their lips and jeer;
  they shake their heads at me (Ps 22:8).

Lesson Four

> ### The Death of Jesus
>
> ³³At noon darkness came over the whole land until three in the afternoon. ³⁴And at three o'clock Jesus cried out in a loud voice, "*Eloi, Eloi, lema sabachthani?*" which is translated, "My God, my God, why have you forsaken me?" ³⁵Some of the bystanders who heard it said, "Look, he is calling Elijah." ³⁶One of them ran, soaked a sponge with wine, put it on a reed, and gave it to him to drink, saying, "Wait, let us see if Elijah comes to take him down." ³⁷Jesus gave a loud cry and breathed his last. ³⁸The veil of the sanctuary was torn in two from top to bottom. ³⁹When the centurion who stood facing him saw how he breathed his last he said, "Truly this man was the Son of God!" ⁴⁰There were also women looking on from a distance. Among them were Mary Magdalene, Mary the mother of
>
> *continue*

one on his left" (15:27), his phrasing reminds the reader that James and John had once asked to be in those positions (10:37). They thought that being on Jesus' right and left would be places of glory. Mark uses the same phrasing here to reveal to his audience the irony of their request. He shows that unwittingly they had asked to be placed in the tradition of suffering servants.

Mark shows Jesus being taunted by everyone present: the passers-by (15:29-30), the chief priests (15:31), and even those crucified with him (15:32). Mark shapes their taunts to underscore the irony of Jesus' plight. The passers-by repeat the earlier false testimony (14:57-58) that Jesus said he "would destroy the temple and rebuild it in three days" (15:29). Both they and the chief priests ironically suggest that he should "save" himself by "coming down from the cross" (15:30, 32). Mark chooses language that reminds his audience that Jesus has said the opposite: "Whoever wishes to come after me must deny himself, take up his cross, and follow me. For whoever wishes to save his life will lose it, but whoever loses his life for my sake and that of the gospel will save it" (8:34-35). The ultimate irony of Mark's narrative lies in the way he shows that in spite of the appearances of death and defeat, Jesus is accomplishing what he set out to do.

The gesture of head-wagging also echoes the mockery of Jerusalem in the Book of Lamentations:

> All who pass by on the road
>   clap their hands at you;
> They hiss and wag their heads (Lam 2:15).

Mark is clearly summoning up a long biblical tradition in which the servants of God are mocked. He interweaves scriptural references into his narrative as a way of communicating the meaning of Jesus' death.

In this context, it is significant that Mark speaks of the title "the king of the Jews" as an "inscription" on Jesus' cross (15:26). It was common Jewish idiom to speak of Scripture as "what is written" or "what is inscribed." Mark thus suggests that the mockery of Jesus is, in its own right, a "Scripture." He sees Jesus' way of the cross as part of the long tradition of righteous prophets and psalmists who suffered for their zeal for God.

When Mark notes that "With him they crucified two revolutionaries, one on his right and

Although the use of **crucifixion** as a method of execution appears to have been known as early as the seventh century B.C.E., its widespread use did not become common until the late fourth century B.C.E. when the practice was spread by Alexander the Great and his successors. The Romans appear to have become aware of crucifixion through their contact with the Carthaginians during the period of the Punic Wars and soon adopted this mode of execution. The Romans used crucifixion to put to death those among the lower classes—slaves, foreigners (especially rebels against Roman rule), and criminals who were convicted of capital crimes. By all accounts, crucifixion was a gruesomely painful way to die, which perhaps explains why the Romans, who crucified prisoners publicly as a deterrent, employed it. While the exact cause of death in crucifixion remains controversial, medical authorities generally agree that shock and impeded respiration leading to asphyxiation were the most likely factors leading to death.

15:33-40 Death

Mark's account of Jesus' death gives details that suggest Creation in the process of being reversed. Light is created at the beginning of Genesis 1; Jesus' death brings darkness (15:33). The loss of light also echoes Jesus' description of the great tribulation, when "the sun will be darkened" (13:24).

Mark next says that Jesus cried out to God (15:34). Significantly, Mark uses Aramaic for the fourth time in the Gospel. The other three times are the raising up of the little girl from death (5:41), the healing of the deaf-mute (7:34), and Jesus' anguished cry to his Father in Gethsemane (14:36)—all key turning points in Mark's Gospel. The words here constitute the opening of Psalm 22, and their significance increases if one knows the whole psalm. It is a psalm in which the speaker begins in despair and moves to an encounter with death, but then is rescued by God, and concludes with thanksgiving and praise. If one knows the whole structure, then the opening verse recalls not only the speaker's initial agony but also his eventual rescue and restoration.

Mark goes on to say that the bystanders are confused by the Aramaic word for "my God" (*Eloi*) and think that Jesus is calling Elijah (15:35). It is worth noting that this is the third time the bystanders have had a place in Mark's account. Each reference indicates a different attitude toward Jesus. The first reference is to Simon of Cyrene, who is forced to help carry the cross (15:21). The second is to the bystanders who revile and taunt Jesus (15:29). In this third reference, the bystanders are simply confused. Their confusion of the word for God with that for Elijah recalls earlier places in Mark's narrative where people confused Jesus' identity with that of Elijah (6:15; 8:28). By repeating the confusion here, Mark suggests that confusion about Jesus' identity remained right up to the end. The episode also serves to clarify the kinship and distinction between Jesus and Elijah. Mark stresses that while Jesus may be like Elijah in many ways, they are not the same.

The next verse repeats the detail, already given in verse 23, of the sour wine offered to Jesus to drink. It is a detail that echoes, as we have noted before, the plight of God's servant in Psalm 69:22. Here this detail is combined with a taunt: "Wait, let us see if Elijah comes to take him down" (15:36). Again the mockery echoes that of the just one in the Wisdom of Solomon:

> Let us see whether his words be true;
>   let us find out what will happen to him in
>   the end.
> For if the just one be the son of God, God will
>   help him
>   and deliver him from the hand of his foes
>   (Wis 2:17-18).

The precise words that Mark uses to describe the moment of Jesus' death are significant: "Then Jesus, releasing a loud voice, breathed out"* (15:37). This literal translation is not as idiomatic as the conventional one, but it serves to highlight Mark's ultimate use of the theme of *release*. When Jesus cures Simon's mother-in-law, Mark says that "the fever *released** her" (1:31b). When Jesus forgives the paralytic, he says, "Your sins are *released*" (2:5). When Jesus heals the deaf-mute, he says in Aramaic, "Be *released*!" (7:34). And we have just seen how Mark shows Pilate ironically releasing a murderous rebel, but not Jesus, from death (15:6, 9, 15). So it is dramatically effective that Mark uses the verb again here, suggesting that Jesus' final breath is freeing.

The splitting of the sanctuary veil (15:38) must be seen in this context. (The translation "torn" is misleading.) The word that Mark uses for "split"* here is an unusual one. He has used

Lesson Four

> the younger James and of Joses, and Salome. [41]These women had followed him when he was in Galilee and ministered to him. There were also many other women who had come up with him to Jerusalem.
>
> ### The Burial of Jesus
>
> [42]When it was already evening, since it was the day of preparation, the day before the sabbath, [43]Joseph of Arimathea, a distinguished member of the council, who was himself awaiting the kingdom of God, came and courageously went to Pilate and asked for the body of Jesus. [44]Pilate was amazed that he was already dead. He summoned the centurion and asked him if Jesus had already died. [45]And when he learned of it from the centurion, he gave the body to Joseph. [46]Having bought a linen cloth, he took him down, wrapped him in the linen cloth and laid him in a tomb that had been hewn out of the rock. Then he rolled a stone against the entrance to the tomb. [47]Mary Magdalene and Mary the mother of Joses watched where he was laid.
>
> *continue*

it once before in his Gospel, when he described the heavens opening up at the moment of Jesus' baptism (1:10). By repeating it here, Mark suggests that a similar event is taking place. In his death, Jesus is opening up the heavens.

This interpretation is strengthened by two details. First, the phrase idiomatically translated here as "top to bottom" is literally "from above to below"*—a wording suggestive of God's creation of the dome of the sky to separate the waters "above" and "below" in Genesis 1:6-8. Second, the unusual word for "split"* is also used in a significant place in the Septuagint (the Greek translation of the Hebrew Bible that the evangelists followed). It appears in a prayer of Isaiah that asks God to split the heavens and come down and take back his sanctuary from Israel's enemies who have trampled it (Isa 63:18–64:1). If we put these details together, we see that Mark's choice of wording suggests that through his death, Jesus is opening up the sacred place of God's dwelling. He is making it accessible.

By immediately following the split veil with the centurion's proclamation of faith in Jesus as "the son of God" (15:39), Mark confirms this understanding. He is suggesting that even the Roman soldier—someone disposed to pollute the Temple with false gods—has come to see the divine image in Jesus' humanity. In his death, Jesus has opened up the heavens even to the Romans.

15:40-41 The watchful women

Before he presents the passion narrative, Mark gives the last word of Jesus to his disciples as "Watch!" (13:37). Mark then shows how Jesus' disciples, particularly his three key disciples, fail to do this (14:32-42). Here Mark introduces a balancing trio of women who do what Jesus has asked. At the same time that Mark shows that all the men have fled (14:50), he also shows that there were women who did not flee but were "seeing* from a distance" (15:40). The verb that Mark uses for "seeing" here is one that implies spiritual insight. The watchful "seeing" of these women stands in contrast to the betrayal by Judas, the denial of Jesus by Peter, and the flight of the other disciples. The women are not labeled "disciples," but Mark describes them acting in the way Jesus has asked his disciples to do. Mark also tells us that they had "followed" Jesus in Galilee and "ministered to him" (15:41a). Mark names three but says there were also many others (15:41b).

The three names that Mark gives are vaguely identified. The first is Mary Magdalene, known in all the Gospels as the first witness to Jesus' resurrection, but not yet called that here. (The idea that she was a "sinful woman" is not in Mark.) The last is Salome, about whom we know nothing. We do know that "Salome" was the name of the daughter of Herodias, who danced for the head of John the Baptist, but in Mark's account of that event, her name is not given (6:17-29). Did Mark assume that his audience knew her name and intended them to infer that she reappears here transformed? The middle woman, described only as "the mother of the younger James and of Joses," is presumably (on the basis of 6:3) the mother of Jesus. It is striking that Mark does not single her out; he treats these women as a generic group. Yet Mark suggests that this generic group of women, in their "following" and "ministering" and, above all, in their watchful "seeing," act in the ways to which Jesus has called all his disciples.

> That the Gospels make mention of **women followers of Jesus**, some of them by name, is just one more indication of the barriers that Jesus overcame as he proclaimed the kingdom of God. Class, race, culture, and gender were seemingly unimportant among the followers of Jesus. We hear of tax collectors, sinners, a member of the Sanhedrin, single women and groups of women, young and old men, the blind and lame, and the hale and hearty—an unheard-of combination in any social institution of the time. The faithfulness of the women is noted or described on more than one occasion. They are with Jesus at his crucifixion when by most accounts his disciples have fled (see Matt 27:55-56; Mark 15:40-41; Luke 23:48-49; John 19:25). Women travel with Jesus and the Twelve and even use their resources to provide for their needs (Luke 8:1-3). Finally, women are among the first to witness the reality of the risen Jesus (Matt 28:1-10; Mark 16:1-11; Luke 24:1-12; John 20:1-18). Their faithfulness placed them near Jesus in all circumstances and challenges us to find ourselves with him too.

15:42-47 Burial

Mark loads every detail of the burial scene with significance. First, he tells us that "it was the day of preparation, the day before the sabbath" (15:42). This is usually understood as just a simple reporting of fact. But given Mark's tendency to emphasize symbolic detail, one might surmise that he wants his readers to consider that the burial of Jesus was "a day of preparation" for his resurrection. The "preparation" theme of chapter 14 is being brought to a climax.

Joseph of Arimathea (15:43) is another disciple hitherto unknown in the Gospel, like the anonymous woman and man at the beginning of chapter 14 (14:3-16). He, like they, appears in the narrative suddenly, just as he is needed. Strikingly, he is described as a member of the council that has just condemned Jesus. His action in asking for the body of Jesus (15:43) suggests a transformation in his understanding of Jesus, just as much as the centurion's proclamation (15:39). Together, the Roman centurion and the Jewish member of the Sanhedrin reverse the judgments of the trials against Jesus.

Mark also characterizes Joseph by saying that he was "awaiting the kingdom of God" (15:43). It is the seventh time that the phrase "kingdom of God" has appeared in Mark's Gospel. The first time is in the preaching of Jesus (1:15). The second, third, and fourth times occur in the chapter containing the seed parables (4:11, 26, 30). The fifth time is when Jesus says approvingly to the scribe, "You are not far from the kingdom of God" (12:34). The sixth time is at the Last Supper, when Jesus says he will "not drink again the fruit of the vine until the day when I drink it new in the kingdom of God" (14:25). "The kingdom of God," in other words, is an important theme throughout the Gospel. When Mark says that Joseph was "awaiting" it, he also picks up on the themes of "watching" and "preparation." Through showing his action of seeking to honor Jesus in death, Mark implies that Joseph now links Jesus with the kingdom.

Pilate's response—wanting to make sure that Jesus was really dead (15:44-45)—confirms the characterization of Pilate that Mark has already given. By means of this detail, Mark again suggests the non-spiritual level on which Pilate exists. In view of Mark's hints of resurrection to come, it is also ironic.

Lesson Four

The linen cloth in which Joseph buries Jesus (15:46) is significant because of the way it recalls the young disciple who left his linen cloth behind when he fled the scene of Jesus' arrest (14:51). The reappearance of a "linen cloth" is suggestive of a restoration. The wrapping of Jesus here in a linen cloth reverses that moment of fear and flight. There is also an echo here of the transformed demoniac, who, after his cure by Jesus, is seen "sitting there clothed and in his right mind" (5:15). That man had "lived among the tombs" (5:5) until his encounter with Jesus changed him. The echo of his story, just as Jesus is being laid in a tomb (15:46), is thus something that gives hope.

Further hope appears in the final detail of the two Marys "watching" where Jesus was laid (15:47). Just as Mark speaks of women "watching" or "seeing"* Jesus' crucifixion, so here he describes women again "watching" where Jesus was buried. Watchful women enclose Mark's narrative of Jesus' burial. Mark says that Joseph "rolled a stone" against the "entrance" or "gate"* to the tomb (15:46). The details together recall Jesus' parable of the man who leaves home and "orders the gatekeeper to be on the watch" (13:34). The two Marys here function as gatekeepers, keeping watch for the lord's return.

Summary of the passion narrative, Part III (15:6-47)

Mark's narrative of Jesus' death is carefully crafted. First of all, Mark weaves his narrative out of echoes and patterns of the Hebrew Bible, telling Jesus' story in the light of them. Second, he picks up earlier themes within his own Gospel, repeating them and making their significance more clear. Third and most important, he constructs a structure of dramatic irony, so that what seems to be leading to Jesus' total doom is in fact moving toward his resurrection.

Mark's use of the Hebrew Bible. The details of Mark's narrative are woven out of numerous images in the Hebrew Bible of "the just one" who is persecuted by powerful and obtuse figures of the world because they do not grasp his identity as God's servant. The primary sources here are Isaiah's "Suffering Servant," sent "like a lamb to the slaughter" by the obtuse kings of the world; the "just one "in the Wisdom of Solomon put to death by "the wicked" because he "boasts that God is his Father"; and the persecuted just one in Psalm 22 who is brought to the point of death and despair before he cries out to God and is rescued. The first two sources provide some of the details for Mark's account of the trial by Pilate and the mockery of the Roman soldiers. Along with Psalm 22, they also provide background for the taunts of Jesus on the cross. Psalm 69 adds the detail of the sour wine given to Jesus in his thirst. All of them offer a pattern or structure that Mark wants his readers to find relevant and illuminating. It is the pattern of God's servant, who appears by the world to be doomed but who in the end is exalted by God. It is this structure of dramatic irony that Mark adopts for his narrative.

Mark's repeating themes. Again and again Mark repeats words or images that recall an earlier place in his Gospel. In each case he uses the echo to give an extra dimension to the present scene, sometimes making it fuller and sometimes pointing up its irony.

When he describes Jesus being mocked by the Roman soldiers, for example, he shows them kneeling before Jesus (15:19). It is a detail that ironically summons up earlier moments in the Gospel when people knelt before Jesus in awe (1:40; 3:11; 5:33).

When Mark tells of someone who is forced to carry Jesus' cross, he notes that he was called "Simon," thus reminding his readers of Simon the leper, who welcomed Jesus into his home (14:3), and Simon Peter, who has just denied him (14:66-72). The echoes intensify the irony of Simon Peter's betrayal.

When Mark describes the crucifixion of Jesus, he notes that the Romans crucified two revolutionaries with him, "one on his right hand and one on his left" (15:27). By his phrasing he ironically recalls the request of James and John for just those positions (10:37).

When Mark quotes Jesus' final death cry, he notes that some thought he was calling Elijah (15:34-35), thus repeating earlier stories of how people were confused about Jesus' identity (6:15; 8:28). The repetition underscores Mark's theme of Jesus' mistaken identity.

When Mark uses the verb "release"* to describe Jesus' death (15:37), he chooses a word that he has associated again and again with Jesus' acts of freeing people from sin and from disease (1:31; 2:5; 7:34). He has also placed it as an ironic refrain in Pilate's mouth, in the context of whether or not he should set Jesus free (15:6, 9, 15). By using it as a description of Jesus' last breath, Mark signals that Jesus' death is a freeing act.

Similarly, by using the same words for "splitting open"* the sanctuary veil (15:38) that he has used to describe the "splitting open" of the heavens at Jesus' baptism (1:10), Mark suggests that Jesus' death is not an end but a beginning.

When Mark describes Joseph of Arimathea "awaiting the kingdom of God" (15:43), he recalls six other mentions of the kingdom (1:15; 4:11, 26, 30; 12:34; 14:25). He thus hints that the kingdom may now be imminent.

When Mark speaks of Joseph wrapping Jesus in a "linen cloth" (15:46), he summons up the stories of the young man who fled (14:51) and the man who had lived "among the tombs" (5:5), whom Jesus transformed (5:15). The echoes provide hope for Jesus' own restoration and transformation.

Mark's dramatic irony. Mark tells the story of Jesus' death and burial in such a way that he alerts the reader to the fact that the plot is really moving in the opposite direction than it appears. He does this both by his echoes of the patterns in the Hebrew Bible and by his use of repeating themes.

Mark also hints at a new beginning by the way he frames the narrative of Jesus' burial with descriptions of women who follow Jesus' instruction to "watch." They remind his readers of Jesus' story of the lord who returns to his house.

CHAPTER 16

The Resurrection of Jesus

¹When the sabbath was over, Mary Magdalene, Mary, the mother of James, and Salome bought spices so that they might go and anoint him. ²Very early when the sun had risen, on the first day of the week, they came to the tomb. ³They were

continue

Summary of the passion narrative, Parts I, II, and III (14:1–15:47)

Part I of Mark's passion narrative focuses on preparations of various kinds. They are ambiguously for both death and life. Part II focuses on Jesus' identity and how he is sentenced because he is mistakenly identified in both his trials. Part III focuses on the dramatic irony of a plot that may seem to be leading to death but is in fact leading to new life.

A NEW BEGINNING: THE RESURRECTION OF JESUS AND THE REVELATION OF WISDOM

Mark 16:1-8

16:1 The women

The same three women who watched Jesus' death (15:40) reappear. Like the anonymous woman at the beginning of chapter 14, they come to anoint the body of Jesus. Mark has shaped his narrative to show that at either end of the passion narrative, there are women coming to anoint Jesus. In Mark's account, their actions claim Jesus as "messiah"—that is, as God's anointed.

16:1-2 The time

Mark says the women came "when the sabbath was over." In Jewish liturgy, a distinction is made between Sabbath time and "ordinary time." The Sabbath is a time set aside to celebrate God and to reflect on his kingdom. The

Lesson Four

> saying to one another, "Who will roll back the stone for us from the entrance to the tomb?" ⁴When they looked up, they saw that the stone had been rolled back; it was very large. ⁵On entering the tomb they saw a young man sitting on the right side, clothed in a white robe, and they were utterly amazed. ⁶He said to them, "Do not be amazed! You seek Jesus of Nazareth, the crucified. He has been raised; he is not here. Behold the place where they laid him. ⁷But go and tell his disciples and Peter, 'He is going before you to Galilee; there you will see him, as he told you.'" ⁸Then they went out and fled from the tomb, seized with trembling and bewilderment. They said nothing to anyone, for they were afraid.
>
> *continue*

other days are time to journey towards this perfect state of being. The Sabbath liturgy concludes with spices to "hallow" and "sweeten" the ordinary days of the week. Mark may have had this concluding prayer in mind when he describes the women bringing spices at the end of the Sabbath. On the literal level, the spices are for burial; on the symbolic level, they may also signify the transition to "ordinary time."

Mark also says they came "very early when the sun had risen, on the first day of the week." Each phrase emphasizes, in a different way, a new beginning.

16:3-4 The stone

The "stone" at "the entrance to the tomb" suggests the sealing off of death from life. When the women say to one another, "Who will roll back the stone for us?" Mark shows their willingness to accept their vulnerability along with their trust that God will provide.

16:5 The young man

The young man "clothed in a white robe" is an angelic figure. The whiteness of his clothing summons to mind the transfiguration of Jesus (9:3), an event that Mark clearly constructed as a foreshadowing of Jesus' resurrection. He also resembles the young man who fled the garden when Jesus was arrested, leaving his linen cloth behind him. The fact that this young man is seen "sitting" also recalls the transformed demoniac, whom the townsfolk found "sitting there clothed and in his right mind" (5:15). Mark's detail about his being "on the right side" further recalls Jesus' proclamation to the high priest that he would "see the Son of Man seated at the right hand of the Power" (14:62). By means of all these echoes, Mark suggests that this young man represents a transformed life.

16:6 The young man's news

The words that Mark quotes the young man as saying form the heart of his Gospel: "You seek Jesus of Nazareth, the crucified. He has been raised; he is not here." The key words are "crucified" and "raised." Throughout his Gospel, Mark has stressed the necessary connection between Jesus and the cross, and between Jesus and resurrection. In Mark's narrative, it is the paradoxical union of those two seemingly contradictory elements that form his identity. Mark shows that both the high priest and Pilate mistake his being called "messiah" as a sign that he sought power. Mark also shows that both mistook his death as the ending of his power. The phrasing here suggests a paradoxical balance: Jesus is both the suffering, crucified one and the one whom God's power has raised up.

16:7a The commissioning of the women

Mark says that the young man told the women to "go forth."* (The verb is stronger than merely "go.") Mark has shown the women acting all along as disciples. By this act of commissioning, Mark suggests that the women are also sent forth as apostles. They are, moreover, sent forth to the male disciples, even to the head disciple, Peter. The women are sent forth to witness to the men.

What are the implications of the role of men and women in Mark's Gospel? Many readers have observed that Mark shows Jesus' male disciples to be obtuse and foolish. Few seem to have noticed that Mark simultaneously shows that Jesus has female disciples who are insightful and wise. If the Gospel is read on a literal, historical level, it is difficult to know what to make of this. But if the Gospel is read on a symbolic level and in the light of the Wisdom traditions, Mark's purpose becomes clear. We have suggested before the extent to which Mark presents Jesus as God's Wisdom made flesh. In the light of the Wisdom writings, Mark characterizes Jesus as a nurturing, healing, compassionate, and maternal figure, always intent on giving and restoring life. Following the same traditions, Mark sets up a typical contrast in his Gospel between the wise and the foolish. There is a creative logic in his choosing women to be like Woman Wisdom, while their male counterparts act out the part of the foolish. Mark also makes the women's raised status and new ministry a symbol of the new creation that Jesus brings into being.

16:7b The message

Mark indicates that the message the women are sent forth to repeat is not about Jesus' glory but about his ministry. It repeats exactly what Mark has shown Jesus saying on the eve of his crucifixion: "But after I have been raised up, I shall go before you to Galilee" (14:28). It confirms his ongoing life: "there you will see him, as he told you." It sends the disciples back to where the Gospel first began. It suggests a new beginning.

16:8 The revelation to the women

The translation given above is conventional, but unfortunately it is badly misleading. The word translated "bewilderment" is *ekstasis* in Greek. Even someone who has never read Greek can see that its English counterpart is "ecstasy."*

The word "ecstasy" literally means "out of [a normal] state [of being]." In the Septuagint (the Greek translation of the Hebrew Bible that the evangelists followed), the word appears at two key moments in the book of Genesis. When God casts Adam into a "deep sleep" or "trance" while he is creating both man and woman (2:21), the word for "trance" is *ekstasis*. Similarly, when God casts Abraham into a "deep sleep" or "trance" while he is making the covenant with him (Gen 15:12), the word for "trance" is *ekstasis*. In both instances, the word conveys the action of God creating something new. It also implies a human being undergoing some shock of transition, a human being experiencing a transformation of consciousness.

Mark uses the word "ecstasy" more than once in his Gospel. When he wants to describe the state of the crowd that witnessed the rising up of the paralytic, he says, "They were all ecstatic and glorified God, saying, 'We have never seen anything like this'" (2:12b). When he wants to describe the changed condition of those who have witnessed Jesus' raising up of Jairus's daughter, he says that "They were out of their minds with ecstasy"* (5:42).

Mark also uses a related word to describe Jesus himself. When he wants to describe how "those close to" Jesus thought he was crazy for mingling so closely with the crowds, he says that they thought he was "out of [his] mind" (3:21).

All these earlier uses of the word support its meaning here. The women are, like Jesus, out of their minds at what they have learned from the angel. And like those who witnessed a paralytic rise up from his mat and a child brought back to life, they are in a state of ecstasy at the realization of Jesus' resurrection. The word conveys that they are undergoing some shock of transition. They are experiencing a transformation of consciousness.

It is a sign of this transformed consciousness that "they went out and fled from the tomb." The foolish (male) disciples fled from Jesus. The wise women follow the example of Jesus and flee from the tomb.

"They said nothing to anyone" because they were in a "trance"—like Adam, like Abraham. By his choice of words, Mark suggests that they were in a state of shock, undergoing a transforming experience. Their silence is more, not less, than words.

They are not silent because "they were afraid." This translation is again conventional but unfortunate. Again, Mark has used the

Lesson Four

word given here twice before in his Gospel—first, to describe the disciples' reaction to Jesus' stilling the storm (4:41), and second, to describe their response to the transfiguration of Jesus (9:6). The NABRE translates the first instance as "filled with great awe" and the second as "terrified." There is no justification for "terrified" because the context is Peter's exclamation that "It is good that we are here!" (9:5). Both contexts suggest the meaning of awe. The context here of "ecstasy" also supports a translation of "awe."

If we put all these pieces together, we would translate Mark's ending as follows:

> And going out, they fled the tomb, for trembling and ecstasy* possessed them, and they said nothing to anyone because they were filled with awe.*

Such a translation would be a fitting conclusion to a Gospel that presents Jesus as Wisdom and the women as faithful disciples of Jesus/Wisdom. Throughout his Gospel, Mark has shown that the women disciples of Jesus not only follow after him but follow his example in serving others. Mark has also shown them to be "watchful," which is the way of Wisdom. He thus prepares his readers for an ending in which they begin to comprehend the revelation that Jesus/Wisdom cannot die but is still alive and in their midst. By showing them overcome by awe, Mark is dramatizing the theme of all the Wisdom writings that "Fear of the Lord is the beginning of Wisdom" (Prov 1:7; 9:10; Sir 1:12, 16; Ps 111:10). That fear is not fright but overwhelmed reverence before the divine mystery.

SUMMARY OF THE DESIGN OF MARK'S GOSPEL

Doublets

We suggested earlier that the two-stage healing of the blind man in 8:22-26 is a key to

The women at the grave of Jesus

the theological design of Mark's Gospel. That is to say, Mark seems to have designed his Gospel in two parts, with the transfiguration in the middle. In the first part (chs. 1–8), the reader is like the blind man who at first only sees "people looking like trees" (8:24). In the second part (chs. 9–16), Mark repeats many of the same images, events, and themes, and the reader now sees them more plainly.

The transfiguration is pivotal because it reveals Jesus' inner glory. We have noted before that Peter's desire to "make three tents" or "booths"* (9:5) suggests the feast of Booths or Succoth, a harvest feast celebrating the end time of God's kingdom. The Markan text says that Jesus "metamorphosed"* before his disciples (9:2), that is, he changed form entirely. Jesus' "dazzling white" garments (9:3) suggest his relationship to other significant figures (for example, Moses and Elijah) who, in popular nonbiblical writing of the time, are imagined ascending to the heavens clothed like angels. In this literary imagination, resurrection and ascension are similar and intertwined events. Thus to a Jewish audience of the time, this scene of Jesus' total transformation and gleaming garments in an end-time setting would have signified his ascension or resurrection from death to a heavenly state. Mark has not placed the scene of Jesus' resurrection at the end of his Gospel but here in the middle, where it illuminates both halves of his Gospel.

The most crucial difference between the two halves lies in Mark's presentation of the identity of Jesus. In the first part, Jesus reflects God's power in miracles of exorcism and healing, stilling the sea and walking on water, and the multiplication of bread. In the second part, Jesus appears vulnerable to the various plottings against him, and he speaks of dispossession, poverty, and death. In the first part, Jesus calls his disciples to be "fishers" on a grand scale (1:17), to preach and cast out demons (3:14-15; 6:12-13a), and to cure the sick (6:13b). But his instructions to them begin to shift radically at the end of chapter 8 when he says, "Whoever wishes to come after me must deny himself, take up his cross, and follow me" (8:34).

The second part of Mark's Gospel leads inexorably to Jesus' taking up his own cross. And Mark's Gospel is often referred to as the one in which "the cross" is key. But by placing the transfiguration at the very center of his narrative, Mark signals that the cross is only one part of the story. The whole story involves *cross plus transfiguration*. In fact, Mark shows that Jesus, in his key statements about the cross, indicates that the cross is *the way* to transfiguration: "For whoever wishes to save his life will lose it, but whoever loses his life for my sake and that of the gospel will save it" (8:35). The cross is not about suffering in itself or suffering for its own sake. The cross symbolizes how God will transform our suffering. God's creative power to transform or transfigure us from suffering humanity into persons of radiant joy is the key to Mark's theology.

In the first part of his Gospel, Mark shows Jesus reaching out to the most alienated and suffering members of his community—those known to be sinners; those possessed by unclean spirits that deprive them of God's holy spirit; those alienated by leprosy or withered limbs; those who are paralyzed; and women of all kinds and ages who, for various reasons, are kept on the fringes of worship. He reaches out in order to "raise them up," to transform their lives. In the second part of his Gospel, Mark shows Jesus himself to be the one who is alienated and suffering, and then Mark tells us Jesus is also "raised up," transfigured (as he has already shown us) by the will of God.

In the first part of his Gospel, Mark shows Jesus as a teacher of Wisdom, speaking in aphorisms and parables or riddles. Yet at the end of chapter 4, as we have seen, Mark indicates that Jesus himself is a living parable or riddle, pointing to what God is like. In the second part of his Gospel, Mark develops this idea, showing that Jesus in suffering, even more than in power, reveals what God is like. Mark indicates this through the image of the split veil of the sanctuary (15:38), suggesting that Jesus, in his dying, has opened up access to God's dwelling. He confirms it in the cry of the centurion, "Truly this was the son of God" (15:39). In that

Lesson Four

cry Mark suggests how, in the dying Jesus, even a Roman soldier came to perceive God's image. Through that perception, Mark challenges his readers to understand how God is reflected even in suffering and dying humanity. Jesus as "son of man" represents us all; Jesus as "son of God" represents us all as made in God's image.

There is a mystery here not easily articulated. The first part of Mark's Gospel is filled with the miraculous; the second part is filled with mystery. Having miraculous powers is what we more readily associate with being God's image. It is difficult to see God's image in suffering and death. But throughout the second part of his Gospel, Mark indicates how Jesus shows and teaches that God reverses our natural expectations and gives us a "second sight," as it were, by which conventional human wisdom is turned upside down.

For example, Jesus surprises those who think that entering God's kingdom requires sophisticated learning, by saying that "whoever does not accept the kingdom of God like a child will not enter it" (10:15). He confounds the normal prizing of wealth by instructing the good, rich man to "Go sell what you have" (10:21). He overturns the normal ambitions for power by instructing his disciples clearly that they are not to "lord it over" others (10:42), but rather, "whoever wishes to be great among you will be your servant; whoever wishes to be first among you will be the slave of all" (10:43-44).

Above all, Jesus rebukes those who think that God's anointed ("messiah") should be immune from suffering and death. In chapter 8, he tells Peter explicitly that this way of thinking is "human-minded" and not "God-minded" (8:33). Then in chapters 14–15, Mark shows Jesus undergoing human suffering and death and somehow revealing God in that very process.

Mark shows that Jesus reveals God even in the process of dying because, at the same time that he shows Jesus being betrayed to his death, he indicates how God will transform that death. In chapter 14, Mark hints at this transformation by the way he describes the anointing of Jesus and by the way he links it to Jesus' last meal, which in turn foreshadows the meal of the Eucharist, itself a meal of transformation.

In chapter 16, Mark indicates the transformation of death through the whole episode of the women coming to the tomb. Through the repeated images of a new day (16:2), he projects a new beginning. Through the images of the stone rolled away (16:4) and the women fleeing from the tomb (16:8), he suggests an escape from death. Through the message of the young man in white (16:6-7), he confirms Jesus' own prediction (14:28) that he would be raised up and return to Galilee. Through his description of the women's silent, awed, ecstatic trance (16:8), he indicates their confrontation with the unexpected, overwhelming power of God to transform death itself into ongoing life.

Triad

Another way of seeing Mark's design is to see the whole Gospel arranged as a triad. First of all, the reader should take note that there are three beginnings. The first is the "beginning" of verse 1, suggesting the very opening of Genesis and the idea of God creating "in Wisdom." The second is the return to "the beginning of creation" in Mark 10:6, which follows upon the transfiguration and introduces Jesus' radical teachings on poverty, powerlessness, and childlikeness. The third is in chapter 16 with its images of a new day and its message of Jesus' return, at what looks like the end, to the beginning of his ministry in Galilee.

From another perspective, there are three sections that each end in a scene of resurrection. The first section, chapters 1–5, concludes with the raising up of the daughter of the synagogue leader Jairus and the image of the witnesses "beside themselves with ecstasy"* (5:42). The second section, chapters 6–9:8, concludes with the scene in which Jesus appears before his disciples transfigured in glory. Here Jesus is pictured in conversation with the great prophets Moses and Elijah, who are also portrayed in a transfigured state. In this scene, the three chief disciples are briefly transfigured too, as Peter seeks to build three harvest "tents" or booths to celebrate the end time, and all three are overcome with awe (9:6). The final section runs from 9:9, when Jesus and his disciples descend the mountain, to 16:8. In 16:6 the three women who have been watching learn that Jesus "has been raised," and transfigured by their new understanding, they are overcome with ecstasy and awe.

In all of these configurations, doublet and triad, the re-creative, transfiguring power of God's Wisdom is at the center.

OTHER ENDINGS BY OTHER AUTHORS

Some time after Mark completed his Gospel, three anonymous authors offered other endings to it. The modern reader may well wonder how anyone had capacity, the desire, or the audacity to do such a thing. They had the capacity because texts were not guarded by copyright laws until fairly recent times. They had the desire because the conventional translation of the last verse of Mark's Gospel made it appear to end in failure. They had the audacity because they regarded themselves as guardians of God's word.

Over the centuries, most commentaries have accepted the idea that the women disobeyed the angel's message because they were shaking with fright. Such a conclusion ignores, of course, the linguistic evidence that Mark uses some form of the word *ekstasis* three times in his Gospel, each time to convey the elevated feelings of those who have witnessed a miracle. It ignores as well the significant use of the word *ekstasis* in the Septuagint to indicate a trance or shift in consciousness induced by God.

It also ignores the linguistic evidence of Mark's use of "awe" to indicate key moments of change in Jesus' disciples—first, to describe their response to Jesus' power to still a violent sea (4:41) and then to describe their response to his transfigured glory (9:6). Its use here forms a typical Markan triad, and its meaning here is illumined by its function in the transfiguration.

Such a conclusion also ignores the role of women throughout the Gospel of Mark: how they are repeatedly "raised up" by Jesus in the first part of the Gospel and how, in the second part, they fulfill the role of true disciples by following, ministering, and "watching," as Jesus has asked. It ignores Mark's use of the Wisdom traditions, where wise people are always contrasted with foolish ones and where Wisdom is portrayed as a woman. Above all, such a conclusion ignores the overall structure of the Gospel, in which God reverses the expected and re-creates all things. If one grasps such a structure, one is open to an ending in which those thought least likely are the ones transformed into witnesses.

It is possible (although not provable) that over the centuries, male leaders in the church have been alarmed at the idea of how a translation using the language of "ecstasy" and "awe" might elevate the role of women. It is possible that male commentators have had a mental block against seeing that while the male disciples in Mark's Gospel are made to look foolish, the female disciples are shown to be wise and faithful witnesses to Jesus' resurrection.

Whatever the cause, the three alternative endings to Mark's Gospel appear in manuscripts known to be faulty. Their dates suggest a limited use by the church. The "Shorter Ending" (see p. 85) is dated somewhere between the seventh and ninth centuries. The third ending (called "The Freer Ending" because it is preserved in the Freer Gallery in Washington, D.C.) is not mentioned before Jerome in the fourth century.

The "Longer Ending" is dated from the second century because it was incorporated into a work of the time (Tatian's *Diatessaron*), but it is not mentioned by either Clement or Origen, significant church fathers of the third and fourth centuries. Tatian's *Diatessaron* was deemed heretical because of its attempt to harmonize all four Gospels. The "Longer Ending" was not made part of the official biblical canon until the Council of Trent in the sixteenth century. It is strange that it was canonized, even though it once formed part of a heretical work, particularly since the ending itself is guilty of trying to blend together different Gospel passages. Even stranger is the fact that although modern scholarship agrees it was not authored

> ### The Longer Ending
>
> #### The Appearance to Mary Magdalene
>
> [⁹When he had risen, early on the first day of the week, he appeared first to Mary Magdalene, out of whom he had driven seven demons. ¹⁰She went and told his companions who were mourning and weeping. ¹¹When they heard that he was alive and had been seen by her, they did not believe.
>
> #### The Appearance to Two Disciples
>
> ¹²After this he appeared in another form to two of them walking along on their way to the country. ¹³They returned and told the others; but they did not believe them either.
>
> #### The Commissioning of the Eleven
>
> ¹⁴[But] later, as the eleven were at table, he appeared to them and rebuked them for their unbelief and hardness of heart because they had not believed those who saw him after he had been raised. ¹⁵He said to them, "Go into the whole world and proclaim the gospel to every creature. ¹⁶Whoever believes and is baptized will be saved; whoever does not believe will be condemned. ¹⁷These signs will accompany those who believe: in my name they will drive out demons, they will speak new languages. ¹⁸They will pick up serpents [with their hands], and if they drink any deadly thing, it will not harm them. They will lay hands on the sick, and they will recover."
>
> *continue*

by Mark, it is still being printed in most Christian Bibles and used by the Catholic Church as the gospel on the Feast of Saint Mark.

Again the question arises as to why the Council made its decision and why the church has continued to honor it. Again the answer seems to lie in the way Mark's original ending has been translated and understood as signifying the women's failure to witness. Were the ending grasped as a description of the women's stunned awe at the realization of Jesus' resurrection, another ending would not be sought.

The Council perhaps justified its choice of this "Longer Ending" because it makes use of passages from Luke and Matthew. It does not seem to have considered, however, whether these borrowings do justice to the Gospels they are taken from or to the rest of the Gospel of Mark. It is important to look at the "Longer Ending" in detail.

THE LONGER ENDING

16:9-11 The appearance to Mary Magdalene

Some commentators have suggested that this verse rehabilitates Mary Magdalene as a witness because she is described here as giving the angel's message to Jesus' "companions." But the description of her as one who had been possessed by "seven demons" (a reference to Luke 8:2) is denigrating. Her speech here, moreover, is ineffective because "they did not believe" her. In the original Markan ending, as we have read it, Mary Magdalene is a witness to the resurrection and an apostle to the apostles. Here she is a former sinner whose words are not given credibility.

16:12-13 The appearance to two disciples

This is a vague reference to Luke's narrative of two disciples encountering the risen Jesus on the road to Emmaus (Luke 24:13-35). Omitted is Luke's development of this narrative into a eucharistic story in which the disciples recognize Jesus "in the breaking of the bread" (Luke 24:35). As it stands, the narrative here goes nowhere.

16:14-16 The commissioning of the Eleven

Jesus' injunction to "Go into the whole world and proclaim the gospel to every creature" comes from the ending of Matthew's Gospel (28:19). The insistence on baptism as the guarantee of salvation, however, is not in Matthew. And such a rigid distinction between the "saved" and the "condemned" is nowhere to be found in Mark.

16:17-18 "Signs will accompany those who believe"

The only two "signs" in the list that appear in the Gospels are the driving out of demons and the laying of hands on the sick. These are mentioned, however, not as "signs" but as ministries. The speaking "in new languages" is not in any of the Gospels, but in Acts and First Corinthians. The power to "tread on serpents" is mentioned in Luke (10:19), but not the power to pick them up. The power to "drink any deadly thing" without harm is nowhere in the New Testament. (And when these words have been taken literally, they have caused death.) In no Gospel does Jesus advocate the seeking of "signs." In fact, there are several places where Jesus rebukes the Pharisees for "seeking a sign" (Mark 8:11-12; Matt 12:38-39; Matt 16:1-4; Luke 11:16).

16:19-20 The ascension of Jesus

The description of Jesus "taken up into heaven" echoes the ending of Luke (24:51). In Luke, it is part of his way of ending the Gospel on a note of expectation. In the same passage, Luke shows Jesus telling his disciples to go to Jerusalem to await "power from on high" (24:49). In the "Longer Ending" there is no such waiting or expectation of the Spirit. Instead, the author tidies things up by saying that the disciples "went forth and preached everywhere while the Lord worked with them."

Summary of the "Longer Ending"

The "Longer Ending" pieces together phrases from other Gospels without doing justice to the way they function in their original contexts. In respect to Mark, if one perceives Mark's Gospel in the terms of this commentary, then the "Longer Ending" appears not only unnecessary but offensive because it clashes with the rest of Mark's Gospel.

As a final reflection, you might want to consider all the ways in which this "Longer Ending" undermines Mark's theological point of view:

The Ascension of Jesus

[19So then the Lord Jesus, after he spoke to them, was taken up into heaven and took his seat at the right hand of God. 20But they went forth and preached everywhere, while the Lord worked with them and confirmed the word through accompanying signs.]

The Shorter Ending

[And they reported all the instructions briefly to Peter's companions. Afterwards Jesus himself, through them, sent forth from east to west the sacred and imperishable proclamation of eternal salvation. Amen.]

—How does it undermine the role of women in Mark's Gospel?

—How does the insistence that "whoever does not believe will be condemned" undermine Mark's focus on Jesus' outreach to sinners, his emphasis on forgiveness, his saying that "Whoever is not against us is for us" (9:40), and his emphasis on God's will and power to transform rather than to condemn?

—How does the emphasis here on "signs" undermine Mark's repeated suggestion that God's kingdom is accessible in ordinary ways?

—How does ending with Jesus' ascension into heaven conflict with Mark's emphasis on Jesus' return to Galilee?

—This ending seems to close off discipleship as a thing of the past instead of opening it up to the future. What effect does that have on you as a reader and potential disciple?

Our commentary raises interesting points about the **"Longer Ending" of Mark's Gospel**, and it is the role of scholars to explore such issues within the sacred text. It is also important to state clearly that **Mark 16:9-20** is part of the

Lesson Four

canonical Gospel of Mark (unlike the later, "Shorter Ending"). It was not uncommon in the ancient world for manuscripts to be edited and developed over time; this development does not in and of itself indicate irresponsibility or manipulative intent. Early interpreters found the original ending (16:1-8) abrupt and/or confusing, even in their reading of the original Greek, and sought to supplement the text with other traditions about the resurrection of Jesus. While one ending is original and the other is a later development, both endings offer something of value; both are regarded by the church as inspired Word of God.

Lesson Four

EXPLORING LESSON FOUR

1. Why did Pilate regard it as dangerous for an Israelite to claim to be "king of the Jews" (15:1-5)?

2. What are some of the ironic factors in the release of Barabbas instead of Jesus (15:6-15)?

3. Simon helped Jesus carry his cross (15:21). In what ways might Christians be asked to help carry Jesus' cross in today's world? (See Col 1:24.)

4. How does the position of the two revolutionaries to the left and right of Jesus (15:27) shed light on an earlier passage in Mark (10:37)?

5. What is the significance of the veil of the sanctuary being torn at Jesus' death (15:38)? (See 1:10; Gen 1:6-8; Exod 36:37-38; Heb 10:19-20.)

Lesson Four

6. Who was Joseph of Arimathea, and how did he assist in Jesus' burial (15:42-47)? (See Luke 23:50-54; John 19:38-42.)

7. Sabin's commentary indicates that the original ending of Mark's Gospel (16:1-8) is in keeping with the rest of the Gospel and is not problematic. However, many readers have found this to be an abrupt and difficult ending. What do you think? What questions, if any, does it pose for you?

8. How does the "Longer Ending" of Mark (16:9-19) pick up on elements found in Luke and Matthew? (See Luke 23:55–24:11, 13-35; Matt 28:16-20.)

9. How has your study of Mark influenced your understanding of Jesus and/or your life as a disciple?

Lesson Four

CLOSING PRAYER

Prayer

When the centurion who stood facing him saw how he breathed his last he said, "Truly this man was the Son of God!" (Mark 15:39)

Jesus, like the centurion who stood before your cross, we believe that you are truly the Son of God. Help us to always openly proclaim our faith in you, without fear or self-consciousness. Today we pray for the grace to bring the good news to others by our words and actions, especially . . .

PRAYING WITH YOUR GROUP

Because we know that the Bible allows us to hear God's voice, prayer provides the context for our study and sharing. By speaking and listening to God and each other, the discussion often grows to more deeply bond us to one another and to God.

At *the beginning and end of each lesson* simple prayers are provided for individual use, and also may be used within the group setting. Most of the closing prayers provided with each lesson relate directly to a theme from that lesson and encourage you to pray together for people and events in your local community.

Of course, there are many ways to center ourselves in God's presence as we gather together in groups around the word of God. We provide some additional suggestions here knowing you and your group will make prayer a priority as part of your gathering. These are simply alternative ways to pray if your group would like to try something different from those prayers provided in the previous pages.

Conversational Prayer

This form of prayer allows for the group members to pray in their own words in a way that is not intimidating. The group leader begins with Step One, inviting all to focus on the presence of Christ among them. After a few moments of quiet, the group leader invites anyone in the group to voice a prayer or two of thanksgiving; once that is complete, then anyone who has personal intentions may pray in their own words for their needs; finally, the group prays for the needs of others.

A suggested process:
In your own words, speak simple and short prayers to allow time for others to add their voices.

Focus on one "step" at a time, not worrying about praying for everything in your mental list at once.

Step One	Visualize Christ. Welcome him. Imagine him present with you in your group. Allow time for some silence.
Step Two	Gratitude opens our hearts. Use simple words such as, "Thank you, Lord, for . . ."
Step Three	Pray for your own needs knowing that others will pray with you. Be specific and honest. Use "I" and "me" language.

Step Four — Pray for others by name, with love.
You may voice your agreement ("Yes, Lord").
End with gratitude for sharing concerns.

Praying Like Ignatius

St. Ignatius Loyola, whose life and ministry are the foundation of the Jesuit community, invites us to enter into Scripture texts in order to experience the scenes, especially scenes of the gospels or other narrative parts of Scripture. Simply put, this is a method of creatively imagining the scene, viewing it from the inside, and asking God to meet you there. Most often, this is a personal form of prayer, but in a group setting, some of its elements can be helpful if you allow time for this process.

A suggested process:

- Select a scene from the chapters in the particular lesson.
- Read that scene out loud in the group, followed by some quiet time.
- Ask group members to place themselves in the scene (as a character, or as an onlooker) so that they can imagine the emotions, responses, and thinking that may have taken place. Notice the details and the tone, and imagine the interaction with the Lord that is taking place.
- Share with the group any insights that came to you in this quiet imagining.
- Allow each person in the group to thank God for some insight and to pray about some request that may have surfaced.

Sacred Reading (or Lectio Divina)

This method of prayer invites us to "listen with the ear of the heart" as St. Benedict's rule would say. We listen to the words and the phrasing, asking God to speak to our innermost being. Again, this method of prayer is most often used in an individual setting but may also be used in an adapted way within a group.

A suggested process:

- Select a scene from the chapters in the particular lesson.
- Read the scene out loud in the group, perhaps two times.
- Ask group members to ponder a word or phrase that stands out to them.
- The group members could then simply speak the word or phrase as a kind of litany of what was meaningful for your group.
- Allow time for more silence to ponder the words that were heard, asking God to reveal to you what message you are meant to hear, how God is speaking to you.
- Follow up with spoken intentions at the close of this group time.

REFLECTING ON SCRIPTURE

Reading Scripture is an opportunity not simply to learn new information but to listen to God who loves you. Pray that the same Holy Spirit who guided the formation of Scripture will inspire you to correctly understand what you read, and empower you to make what you read a part of your life.

The inspired word of God contains layers of meaning. As you make your way through passages of Scripture, whether studying a book of the Bible or focusing on a biblical theme, you may find it helpful to ask yourself these four questions:

What does the Scripture passage say?
Read the passage slowly and reflectively. Become familiar with it. If the passage you are reading is a narrative, carefully observe the characters and the plot. Use your imagination to picture the scene or enter into it.

What does the Scripture passage mean?
Read the footnotes in your Bible and the commentary provided to help you understand what the sacred writers intended and what God wants to communicate by means of their words.

What does the Scripture passage mean to me?
Meditate on the passage. God's word is living and powerful. What is God saying to you? How does the Scripture passage apply to your life today?

What am I going to do about it?
Try to discover how God may be challenging you in this passage. An encounter with God contains a challenge to know God's will and follow it more closely in daily life. Ask the Holy Spirit to inspire not only your mind but your life with this living word.